40 Coast and Country Walks

The author and publisher have made every effort to ensure that the information in this publication is accurate, and accept no responsibility whatsoever for any loss, injury or inconvenience experienced by any person or persons whilst using this book.

published by
pocket mountains ltd
The Old Church, Annanside, Moffat, DG10 9HB
pocketmountains.com

ISBN: 978-1-907025-53-2

Printed in Poland

Introduction

From the crumbly rhubarb-and-cream-coloured cliffs of the Jurassic Coast in the southeast to the surf-stroked craggy coves in the north, across the wilderness and woodlands of Dartmoor and Exmoor, and through the verdant valleys and great green grazing lands of the dairy belt – Devon is a county of exquisite contrasts and natural wonder.

This is nirvana for walkers of all ages and abilities. Whether you're looking for an easy afternoon stroll along the shore, a riverside ramble to an atmospheric country pub or a tor-topping trek on the moors, there's something to suit every boot.

History

Those who like their hikes to have a historical backdrop are particularly well served here, with headlands and hilltops offering a series of forts, castles and defensive structures, some dating from prehistoric tribal times, others a remnant of more modern scuffles with our near neighbours. The Spanish Armada cruised right along this coast, with Sir Francis Drake and co in hot pursuit, and the cliffs are fringed with forts, gun batteries and lookouts from the Napoleonic Wars and the Second World War.

Even inland, you will come across ancient hillforts – some from the Iron Age, others of Roman, medieval or Civil War origin – and Second World War pillboxes. Many of the latter form part of the Stop Line, a defensive boundary created between the Bristol Channel and Seaton – following the evacuation of Allied troops from Dunkirk during the Second World War – to protect the rest of England in the event of an enemy land invasion of Devon and Cornwall (where the coast was considered almost too extensive and wild to be defendable).

Successful attacks on England had come this way before. William of Orange landed at Brixham on his way to dethroning James II during the Glorious Revolution in 1688, just a few years after the Duke of Monmouth led a less successful attempt at toppling the king by sailing into Lyme Bay and whipping up a revolt.

A twisted tangle of inlets, estuaries and bays – some savagely serrated and lined with snarling rocky teeth – the Devon coastline on either side of the county is a joy for walkers, but often a perilous place for sailors. Both shores are littered with the wrecks of ships that have floundered in times of war and peace, across hundreds of years of seafaring activity, which has included plenty of piracy and other salty shenanigans. The coves and caves that punctuate the peninsulas have certainly been well used by smugglers down the centuries, and folk songs and stories recounted on the walls and in the bars of ancient pubs in fishing villages all across Devon keep such maritime memories alive.

Wildlife

Around the beaches and bays of the north coast and the South Hams, curious seals fish and frolic amongst the rocks, dolphins do regular swim-bys and basking sharks – and even the odd sunfish – can occasionally be spotted from the cliffs above.

It's a feather-filled heaven for twitching trekkers. The wetlands and estuaries of the south coast boast cacophonous populations of wading birds, and this is the first port of call for many migratory species making their way north from continental Europe and Africa. The South Hams is one of the last refuges of the endangered little cirl bunting, and raptors from kestrels to peregrine falcons soar high above the heathlands.

The moors are populated by wild ponies, an evocative sight in the dawn mist when you're out for a morning meander. In the woodlands, deer, foxes and badgers can also be seen, and lucky walkers might catch a glimpse of an otter on the riverbanks – or even a wild beaver, now that the species has staged an unlikely comeback on the River Otter, several hundred years after the resident English population was annihilated.

Conditions

The climate here varies almost as much as the terrain. You need to be prepared for anything on Dartmoor, where conditions can turn extremely challenging in the blink of an eye, but generally speaking

temperatures are relatively warm in this part of England compared to walking destinations further north. Rain, of course, is no stranger to these shores – those near-luminous green fields that provide such lush fodder for the Devon dairy industry are well watered by the elements – but sun-drenched summer days are plentiful too.

This eclectic selection of walks, rambles, hikes, treks and dawdles reflects the astonishing diversity of Devon's topographic offering. Each is worth doing multiple times, because they change so completely with the turning of the seasons. On one wander you might find yourself wading through a high tide of bluebells, and the next time you'll be showered with a colourful confetti of autumn leaves.

None of these walks demand a huge degree of fitness, but Devon is undeniably a county of curvy contours and voluptuous valleys, and hills are the common denominator. As walkers, you know that the high ground is where the best views live, and we're not talking mountaineering here – just ambling ascents of bucolic bumps. So dump an extra dollop of jam on your scone (after the clotted cream, always...), lace your best boots up and get stuck in.

The Jurassic Coast

A strangely under-visited part of Devon is the sensational stretch of World

Heritage-listed coastline that faces the English Channel on its southern flank. People typically associate the Jurassic Coast with Dorset, but this natural wonder doesn't stop at the county line in Lyme Regis, it continues in a glorious arc of fossil-strewn beaches and colourful cliffs right around Lyme Bay to Exmouth, and the section between the estuaries of the Axe and the Exe is arguably the most interesting of all.

Here, while exploring sections of the epic South West Coast Path, you can walk back in time through 185 million years of geological activity, spanning almost the entire Mesozoic Era (also known as the Age of Reptiles). Trek from the Triassic, through the Jurassic to arrive at the Cretaceous, when the rockstar generation of dinosaurs – including T-Rex – was teetering on the edge of oblivion.

Ruby-tinted Triassic-era cliffs, formed when England was an arid and landlocked region close to the equator, 200 to 245 million years ago, can be seen all along the East Devon coast, but most spectacularly around Sidmouth and during a walk that leads along the headland and the mouth of the River Otter.

Thanks to an ancient fault line at Seaton Hole – which turned a section of this coast's topography on its head – Seaton is the only place along the entire Jurassic Coast where evidence of all three of these geological eras can be seen simultaneously. Here you can stand on the pebbly beach and observe classic Triassic-coloured cliffs to your left and immediate right – but you can also take in the great white walls that make up Beer Head, laid down during the Cretaceous era (145 to 66 million years ago), when this spot formed the seabed beneath a tropical ocean.

The opening of the Seaton Jurassic

Centre in 2016 has started to magnify this region's presence on the map, but the walking paths remain unruffled by crowds and can often be enjoyed in glorious solitude.

How to use this guide

The 40 walks in this guidebook range from 3km to 17.5km in length. Most are perfect for a morning mooch or an afternoon amble, but some – including the big daddy of the lot, the Bovey Valley adventure across a slice of wild Dartmoor – offer a slightly more serious challenge and are best done when you've got a full day to dedicate to the experience.

Between them, these trails will take you on a rollercoaster ride across moors and up tors, over headlands and hilltops, through wild woodlands, along serpentine rivers and down combes to cute coves and secret beaches. Without exception, your effort will be richly rewarded with stunning coast and country vistas, secluded picnic spots, surprise wildlife encounters and unforgettable experiences.

Several well-signposted long-distance footpaths thread through the county – including the epic South West Coast Path, the Tarka Trail, the Two Moors Trail and the

West and East Devon Ways. The walks in this guide touch on many of these routes, and paths are generally easy to follow with decent underfoot terrain. But be aware that conditions can change quickly – especially on Dartmoor – and routes can be tougher than they appear on paper, particularly when it's wet and muddy.

Each route is accompanied by a sketch map, showing key topographical features of the area you will be walking through, but these should not be relied upon for navigation – the Ordnance Survey (OS) maps are best for this purpose. The relevant 1:25,000 OS map has been highlighted in the introductory text to each walk (except where the route spans two map sheets, when the 1:50,000 map is sometimes recommended instead).

An estimated time allowance has also been provided for each route – this is a rough guide only and will obviously vary according to numerous factors, including conditions underfoot, your walking speed and how many viewpoints (or pubs) you stop at along the way.

These walks are primarily circuits or return routes. Details of how to catch public transport to the start point is provided wherever possible, alongside parking information, but be aware that some regional bus services do not run particularly regularly – especially out of season. Parking areas usually cost, but National Trust members can often take advantage of National Trust–managed car parks for free.

Strong winds can occur throughout the year right across Devon. Take care around clifftops, which are very rarely fenced off and can often plunge dramatically to rocks below, just metres from the path. This is especially important when walking with children. Be sure to carry adequate warm and waterproof clothing, as well as drinking water. Mobile phone reception is patchy in the more remote areas.

Dogs are welcome on most paths, as long as they are under control and do not pose a threat to sheep, cattle or wildlife. Always look out for signage, however, as some areas (such as Seaton Wetlands) do not allow dogs due to the fragility of the ecosystem.

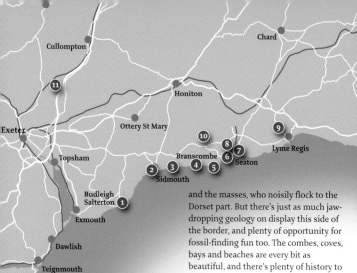

and the masses, who noisily flock to the Dorset part. But there's just as much jaw-dropping geology on display this side of the border, and plenty of opportunity for fossil-finding fun too. The combes, coves, bays and beaches are every bit as beautiful, and there's plenty of history to explore, from Second World War defences to Tudor houses and Iron Age hillforts.

For walkers, East Devon's under-the-radar image is a bonus, leaving many of the myriad tracks and trails that thread through the coast and hinterland gloriously untrammelled even in the height of the season.

The 2016 opening of the impressive Seaton Jurassic Discovery Centre is awakening interest in this hidden corner, however, transforming the town into a real regional hub, where visitors can get information about walks all around the area, from the wonderful wetlands that extend up the River Axe estuary right behind the centre to the clifftop paths that wend their way along the coast in both directions.

This is the time to go and discover what makes East Devon's heart tick – before word really gets out…

Entering Devon from Dorset, you pierce straight to the green heart of arguably England's most bucolically picturesque county, where grazing fields – lush to the point of near-luminosity – roll right to the very edge of strikingly colourful cliffs along a breathtaking coastline that has earned a World Heritage listing for the natural treasures it offers.

Perhaps because it's a little further flung, the Devon half of the Jurassic Coast has long been overlooked by the media

8

East Devon

Brandy Head and the River Otter

Distance 10.5km Time 3 hours 30
Terrain coastal and clifftop paths,
riverside trails, quiet country lanes and
some pavement Map OS Explorer 115
Access bus (157) from Exmouth and
Sidmouth to Otterton; parking at Ladram
Bay Holiday Park (parking charge)

**This looping route takes in every element
of the landscape that makes East Devon
truly an area of outstanding beauty, from
the tan-coloured Triassic-era cliffs that
rise so abruptly from the churning
channel to the beguiling banks of the
River Otter and the charming antiquity of
Otterton, an unassuming village with a
history stretching to Saxon times.**

The walk starts in the sprawling and
sometimes super-busy surrounds of
Ladram Bay Holiday Park, but you'll soon
leave the crowds behind on the South
West Coast Path, which dissects the park.
One arm leads east to Sidmouth and the
other goes west towards Budleigh

Salterton. You want the latter, so turn
right and walk with the sea on your left.

After climbing the grassy hill to reach
Smallstones Point, turn to look back at
Sidmouth across the red heads of Hern
Point and Big Picket Rocks, then continue
around the curve of Chiselbury Bay and
over Crab Ledge to reach Brandy Head.

This place earned its boozy name from
the firewater commonly smuggled in
under cloak of darkness along this
coastline, far from the officious eyes of
the customs men. During the Second
World War, an observation point stood
here, and the RAF also used the head for
target practice when testing new
weaponry. Typhoons, Hurricanes and
Spitfires would roar over the cliffs to let
loose at land- and sea-based targets with
their mounted guns. Anecdotally, local
lads from Otterton would risk life and
limb by hiding to watch this action
unfold, and decades later scuba divers
were recovering ordnance (non-sea shells)

◄ Otter Estuary

from the water below, to sell at Ladram Bay.

Continue to Black Head and Danger Point – taking care around the clifftops, which plunge vertically to the rocks below – and descend towards the seaside resort town of Budleigh Salterton, which sits on the far bank of the River Otter.

Turn right at the river and follow the path up the estuary, a haven for birdlife. After about 500m, eagle-eyed amblers will spot a discreet hide tucked into the trees on the left, with an excellent view of the mouth and mudflats. Glamorous visitors include the glossy ibis, but you can often spot egrets and herons here, along with redwings, fieldfares, nightjars and peregrine falcons, which patrol the cliffs.

A further 500m on, cross a bridge and turn right to walk along the wonderful west bank of the Otter. The waterway is home to otters – although the animals are both rare and shy, having suffered terribly at human hands. In 2013, a breeding pair of wild beavers mysteriously appeared on this river, the first of their species to make a go of it in England since they were hunted to oblivion in the 16th century.

Continue on this bank, ignoring Clamour Bridge (a footbridge), until you reach and cross the bridge at Otterton. Go past a working watermill, which is more than 1000 years old, and a distinctive church on your right, and walk up Fore Street. When the road forks, take Bell Street (right), and then turn right again to climb a hill towards Monks Wall where, in the 12th century, a priory once stood. Here, a track leads towards the sea. When you meet the South West Coast Path, turn left and retrace your steps to Ladram Bay.

11

Sidmouth and The Byes

Distance 7km Time 3 hours
Terrain riverside footpaths, park trails,
beachside esplanade Map OS Explorer 115
Access car parking by Sidford Rugby Club
on Byes Lane (free) or at Church Street
car park (small charge); Sidford is served
by several buses

Created to provide protection for local
wildlife, The Byes is a green ribbon of
river-hugging parkland, fields and
footpaths that wends and bends from
the village of Sidford to the Old
Tollhouse in Sidmouth.

Booting along the Byes is a regular
Sunday afternoon adventure for local
families and this walk is an excellent way
to explore Devon's shortest river: the
lovely little Sid, which flows just 10km
from its source before meeting the
Channel in the classic English seaside
resort of Sidmouth.

Join the route by the Rugby Club on
Byes Lane, where walkers and cyclists
share the path. Stroll south, passing
Sidmouth College on your right.
Surrounded by clumps of trees at every
turn, the serpentine Sid slides through
fields to your left. The path winds around
wildflower-splattered Gilchrist Field
nature reserve, then skirts the edge of
Margaret's Meadow, a more manicured
open area, home to a stunning oak tree.

A little further on you finally meet Sid
properly. The excited river rushes over a
weir here, and you can cross the water via
a wooden bridge, but walk on, with the
river on your left, as the cycling and
walking tracks diverge for a distance.
Continue through a park punctuated by
beech, sycamore, chestnut and weeping
willow trees, keeping your peepers peeled
for kingfishers.

Pass another bridge (where the cycle

◀ The Clock Tower

route hops banks), and then use the third bridge to cross the Sid. Turn right and carry on until you meet a gate leading out onto Salcombe Road, next to the historic 19th-century Byes Toll House.

Carefully cross the road and continue down Mill Street – which suddenly bears right and crosses the river via a ford and bridge – then take the next left along Riverside Road. This leads to a children's play park overlooking the Sid as it meets the red face of Salcombe Hill and cruises past the ruddy cliffs to join the sea.

Sidmouth is a charismatic holiday spot that's been popular with seafront-seeking city dwellers since the Napoleonic Wars made going to the continent problematic for the English gentry.

Grab an ice cream and wander along the front, passing rows of Regency buildings on your right. At the end of the Esplanade, the South West Coast Path shimmies around the ankles of Peak Hill, the path almost becoming a tunnel beneath the cliff's furrowed frown.

Here, two sets of steep steps ascend to the Clock Tower cakery and restaurant, with Jacob's Ladder being the easiest option. At the top, enjoy views of Peak Hill proper and the wilder western half of Sidmouth Beach, before exploring Connaught Gardens, a walled area full of exotic trees, which forms a peaceful

sanctuary (despite a disturbing tale of murder spelt out on a blue wall plaque).

Leave the gardens and return to the Esplanade via Peak Hill Road. Walk along the seafront to the corner of Old Fore Street, where the Dukes Inn sprawls. Turn left here and wander through the pretty town, taking Dove Lane to Fore Street, going left and then right along East Street to The Ham by the river.

Head back past the ford and along the Sid, staying on the eastern bank of the river this time, to explore new turf. At the third bridge, cross and retrace your footsteps to Sidford.

13

Wild Weston donkey trek

Distance 4km Time 1 hour 30
Terrain woodland tracks, coast path,
beach, country lanes Map OS Explorer 115
Access bus (899) from Seaton and
Sidmouth to the Donkey Sanctuary;
parking at the Donkey Sanctuary (free)

This scenic trot through a verdant valley
to a stunning and secluded cliff-backed
beach begins and ends at the Donkey
Sanctuary near Sidmouth. This is the
mothership of an extraordinary charity
that, since 1969, has taken in tens of
thousands of abused, neglected and
unwanted donkeys from across Britain
and Ireland, and has improved the lives
of the often ill-treated animal all around
the world.

The sanctuary sprawls over a vast
amount of land, which extends right
down to the coast and is criss-crossed
with excellent walking trails, all open to
the public, including a section of the
South West Coast Path. Parking is free, as
is entry to the sanctuary itself (donations
welcome), where there's plenty to see and
do, such as donkey grooming. Post-walk,
the Hayloft Restaurant provides a
welcome manger for grazing and lazing.

From the car park, walk into the
sanctuary, past the visitor centre, and
enter the main yard, where you can meet
some of the equine inhabitants in the big
barn. Pass through a gate at the bottom
right corner, go straight ahead and then
turn right through a gate to begin the
walk proper, the first part of which
shadows the sanctuary's 'D Walk', colour
coded green.

The path descends through the 'Field of
Dreams', with dense woods on either side
of the steeply sloping meadow, where

you can enjoy wildflowers such as purple loosestrife, ragged robin and red campion. Follow the well-defined Dunscombe track as it drops down, crossing stiles and wending through fields, until you reach a gate at the top of the cliffs, where the coast path is signposted.

Go through the gate and descend a set of steps to Weston Beach. This pebbly seashore is something of a secret spot, used by local families, dog walkers and – just so you know – the very occasional naturist.

A stream cuts across the beach, making it a perfect dam-building spot for big and little kids, and the wild swimming is great (obviously there's no lifeguard, so go in at your own risk). In both directions the beach is flanked by the red cliffs that are so iconic along this often-forgotten but ever-excellent stretch of the Jurassic Coast.

Stay and play for as long as you like, but when you're ready to go, look for the path leading up the hill on the opposite side of the stream to the one you arrived on. Climb the right shoulder of the valley, Weston Combe, which is slightly less steep than the one you descended. Follow

the path as it bears right and meets the road at Weston.

Turn left onto Grammar Lane, and then left again onto Slade Lane, which takes you back onto Donkey Sanctuary property. A path, signposted as 'C Walk' (purple) runs along the inside of the hedge to the right of this lane, so you can walk next to the donkey fields instead of on the road. Follow this back into the main part of the sanctuary.

◀ Donkey Sanctuary coastline

Branscombe circular

Distance 5.5km Time 2 hours
Terrain coast path, woodland tracks,
country lanes, steps Map OS Explorer 115
Access bus (899) from Seaton and
Sidmouth to Branscombe; parking at
Branscombe Mouth (parking charge)

Branscombe is often said to be England's
longest village, and this rambling route
seems to support this claim. To be fair,
it's more a collection of hamlets linked
by a serpentine stream than one distinct
village, but Branscombe boasts its own
brewery and a couple of Devon's finest
pubs, so we won't quibble.

On top of being long, Branscombe is
also lumpy. The hills here are proper
beasts, but don't worry, the steepest bit
is saved for the downhill return.

From the car park at Branscombe
Mouth, cross the stream via the ford-side
footbridge to reach the beach (site of a
modern shipwreck). Turn right and take
the path away from the sea, to the left of
the Sea Shanty beach café. Ignore the path
going hard left up the hill, and instead go
straight forward on a level track.

This trail leads around the car park
and bears right, crossing the stream via
another footbridge. At a fork, stay left
(the right-hand turn leads to the
Mason's Arms, so-named because of
the stonemasons that lived here and
worked in nearby Beer Quarry Caves,
which have supplied much-coveted
masonry to many famous buildings,
including St Paul's, Winchester and
Exeter Cathedrals).

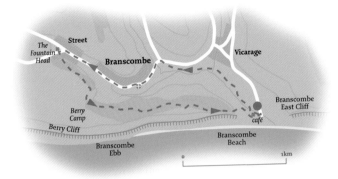

The path goes against the flow of the stream, which rushes towards the beach, chased along by the contours of the great green hill that lies off to your left, waiting to introduce itself properly on the return leg. By some buildings, the path goes through a gate and becomes a lane, and you'll soon emerge at the Old Bakery (complete with wood-fired ovens), historic mill and thatched forge, which dates to Norman times and is still very much in operation. These are all run by the National Trust.

Turn left along the road and walk up to the 12th-century church of Saint Winifred, which occupies a spot with even older Saxon-era heritage. Not far past the church you'll pass an extraordinary garden on your left, which belongs to a house on the other side of the road. Doreen's Garden is a perpetual explosion of colour and life, and is populated by various stone animals that get kids excited. You're welcome to enter and look around, but she would love you to make a donation, which all goes to the Devon Air Ambulance Trust.

Make a final push up the hill to reach the Fountain Head pub and enjoy the low-ceiling, gigantic-fireplace atmosphere of this 14th-century inn, built on the site of a spring (hence the name), and complete with its own ghost. The bar sells good food and excellent ales from the brewery just down the road.

Suitably refreshed, leave the pub, turning right as you exit the door, and look for the signposted footpath leading up the hill. At the top of a stern climb, amid the surrounds of an Iron Age fort at Berry Camp, you'll meet the South West Coast Path. Turn left and follow the footpath across the spine of the hill until you emerge from the trees to see Branscombe Mouth lazily yawning below, beside a sparkling sea.

Mind your footing on this final descent; if you stumble and gain momentum, you won't stop until you hit the Sea Shanty...

◀ The Fountain Head

Branscombe Beach from Beer

Distance 5.5km **Time** 2 hours
Terrain coast path, headland tracks,
country lanes, pebbly beach, steps
Map OS Explorer 115 and 116 **Access** bus
(899) from Seaton and Sidmouth to Beer;
parking at Beer Head (parking charge
from April to October)

Linking two of the Jurassic Coast's
most popular villages, this route takes
walkers on a classic adventure as the
South West Coast Path dramatically
dances over the undulating clifftop
carpet of green grazing land that extends
between Beer and Branscombe, before
dropping down to beach level and
returning along the undercliffs.

From the Common Hill car park at the
top of the hill, just southwest of Beer, exit
on the inland side and turn left up the
road, walking past the caravan park. Follow
the lane as it forks left, crosses a cattle grid

and heads towards an old, lonely-looking
coastguard house, long retired but still
staring dutifully out to sea. During the
Second World War, this part of the
headland was home to an RAF radar
station, part of the Chain Home Low
system designed to detect the approach of
low-flying enemy aircraft.

Go around the coastguard building, and
keep heading west. Shortly after passing
through a gate, the path tumbles down a
set of steep wooden steps leading to a
meadow, which also drops sharply. In the
bottom left corner of this field is an old
Second World War pillbox. Go through the
nearby gate and cross the stream to reach
the beach. The Sea Shanty café sells
emergency ice creams and coffees here.

In 2007, Branscombe Mouth was the
scene of great excitement, when the
merchant ship *MSC Napoli* was wrecked
not far offshore, spilling its cargo and
causing the biggest influx of
opportunistic treasure hunters seen since
smuggling was all the rage here. An
enormous anchor, donated to the village
by the *Napoli*'s red-faced owners, is a
reminder of the disaster.

From the anchor, looking at the sea, turn left onto the beach and walk across the pebbles, past several beach shacks built into the undercliffs on your left. After a crunching 1km, stick close to the scrub at the top of Hooken Beach and look closely for the entrance to the lower path. The gap appears from nowhere shortly before you reach the Pinnacles, towering chalk stacks that have stood aloof from the rest of the cliffs since an 18th-century landslide estranged them.

It's no accident that the entrance to the Underhooken is tricky to locate. This area saw plenty of smuggling shenanigans several centuries ago, with an 1807 report making particular reference to contraband being stashed in the gorse bushes here.

Follow the path as it twists and turns through the Underhooken undergrowth and then darts up a set of leg- and lung-busting steps to the top of the cliff. As you pause to catch your breath during the ascent, look around and inhale the extraordinary vistas that surround this idyllic spot.

At the top, turn right and trace the South West Coast Path back towards Beer Head, taking the cliff-hugging route this time to get a good eyeful of the English Channel. The quality of the view here was put to practical use during the latter years of the 18th century, when a substantial ten-gun artillery battery was positioned on Beer Head in case of attack from Napoleon's France. One night, some of the guns plunged into the sea during a cliff collapse.

With this in mind, don't stray too close to the edge as you round the head and circle the holiday park to arrive back at the car park.

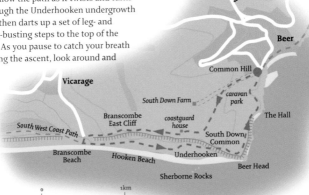

Seaton's Jurassic classic

Distance **7km** Time **3 hours** Terrain **coast path, woodland tracks, country lanes and village streets** Map **OS Explorer 116** Access **bus (885) from Axminster Train Station and (52 or X9) from Exeter to Seaton; parking at the Seaton Jurassic Discovery Centre**

The 2016 opening of the excellent Seaton Jurassic Discovery Centre, where this walk starts and finishes, has helped highlight the treasures the often-overlooked Devon half of the Jurassic Coast offers by the bucketload.

The centre is perfectly positioned too, since Seaton is the only place along the whole World Heritage–listed coast where you can see evidence of the three periods that define this natural wonder (Triassic, Jurassic and Cretaceous) all together, as this route reveals. The walk takes in sections of the South West Coast Path and leads to Beer, one of Devon's most delightful villages and the perfect place to have a half-time ale before heading home.

From the Discovery Centre, stroll down to the wide seafront. Look left across the pebbly beach and beyond the mouth of the River Axe to see the distinctive red cliffs, which lead around to Lyme Regis; their coloration comes from the Triassic period, when England was shifting away from the equator. Look right and you'll see another stretch of red rocky wall, but beyond a gap known as Seaton Hole – an ancient fault line – the cliffs turn bright white. This chalky headland, which you're about to walk across, was formed when England was mostly underwater during the Jurassic and Cretaceous periods.

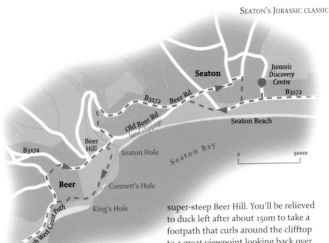

Start walking up Castle Hill, and follow the footpath as it bends left away from the road. Enter Cliff Field Gardens through a gate on your right and check out the timeline that borders the path, walking you through the birth of Planet Earth and continuing your geological education.

Leave the park and turn left on Beer Road. The South West Coast Path once ran along Old Beer Road (next left) but a land slippage has closed this street, so stay on (new) Beer Road all the way over the brow of the hill until you reach a sign pointing left to a permissive path leading through a small clump of woods. Take this path and descend to Old Beer Road (you're now beyond the slippage area), where you turn left.

At Seaton Hole (where there's a café and fossil-rich beach), turn right and climb super-steep Beer Hill. You'll be relieved to duck left after about 15m to take a footpath that curls around the clifftop to a great viewpoint looking back over Seaton and the aforementioned red cliffs.

Stick to this path as it wends its way over the hill to the fabulous fishing village of Beer, a view of which opens up soon after the summit. Take the steps down to The Anchor Inn (with a superb beer garden), and follow the slipway to the beach if you think you'll have the energy to get back up.

Wander through the postcard-pretty village, which has a stream running through it, and turn right at the church to climb a steep alleyway. At the top, turn right, watching out for traffic, and take the path that skirts the road to the top of Beer Hill. Walk down, passing the junction where you turned off earlier. Turn left at the bottom and retrace your steps into Seaton, either going via Cliff Field Gardens again or staying on Beer Road to head through the town and along its attractive high street.

◀ Beer view

The Axe and the Coly

Distance 7km Time 3 hours 30 (one way)
Terrain riverside paths, wetland trails,
country lanes and village streets
Map OS Explorer 116 Access bus (885)
from Axminster and (52 or X9) from
Exeter to Seaton; return by the tourist
tram or bus (885) from Colyton to Seaton;
parking at the Jurassic Discovery Centre

A tale of two rivers, this walk begins by
wending through the wetlands that
fringe the tidal estuary of the Axe.
Passing through the village of Colyford it
then takes you on a riverside ramble
along the banks of the Coly, into the
rebellious heart of Colyton.

You can make this walk shorter by
walking in one direction and catching the
charismatic tram in Colyton to trundle
back in style along the old London and
South Western Railway branch line which
follows a scenic route into Seaton, right
through the ever-changing wetlands.

The Seaton Jurassic Discovery
Centre, run by the Devon Wildlife Trust,
provides plenty of information about
the wetlands and riverbanks you're
about to explore. From here, walk north
along the Underfleet and turn right
onto a path, passing a children's play
area on your right.

Go past the Kings Arms beer garden
(with resident alpacas) and St Gregory's
Church on your left. The River Axe was
once a much wider waterway, navigable by
large ships, and this church enjoyed a
riverbank location when it was built in
the 12th century.

The path then bends left and meets
Colyford Road. Turn right and walk along
the pavement (which swaps sides) until
you see Seaton cemetery on your right.
Carefully cross the road, pass through the
graveyard and turn left into the wetlands
at Black Hole Marsh. (Note: dogs are not
allowed on this section.)

Punctuated by bird hides – most perched in the midst of the avian action, accessed by stilted walkways – the wetlands offers sightings of hundreds of species of migratory and wading birds. This section is a mecca for twitchy trekkers when the tide's out, but it's prettiest when the water is high. There are great views across the river to Axmouth, and the trail also forms part of the Stop Line Way, a work-in-progress cycling and walking route that follows a line of Second World War defences, built as a cut-off point in case Devon and Cornwall were invaded.

The path exits the wetlands at Colyford Common. Turn left before the circular reedbed walk to take a track to the road, where you go right and walk into the village. Take another right at the T-junction, pass the Wheelwright Inn on your left, carefully negotiate the pavement-free corner to the bridge across the Coly and turn left through a gate to join a footpath opposite the White Hart Inn.

This scenic path traces the beautiful banks of the River Coly for the next 1.5km. Ignore the first bridge, but cross the second one, then walk with the river on your right until you reach a gate leading into a small business yard.

Here, go left to explore historic Colyton, known as Devon's rebel town since the 17th century, when locals fatefully sided with the Duke of Monmouth, who had landed at Lyme Regis in June 1685 to whip up support for a rebellion against his Catholic uncle James II. Monmouth was walloped at the Battle of Sedgemoor and 'Hanging Judge Jeffreys' sentenced most survivors to swing in the 'Bloody Assizes' held around the region.

Return along Station Road, bearing right after crossing the river and then turning left to reach the Tramway Station, where you can hitch a unique ride back to Seaton. Alternatively, retrace your steps along the river and through the wetlands.

◀ Seaton Wetlands hide

Holyford Woods

Distance 3km **Time** 1 hour
Terrain woodland trails
Map OS Explorer 116 **Access** bus (885)
from Axminster and (X9) from Exeter to
Seaton; parking at the top of Seaton
Down Road

A short stroll, this rural ramble
nevertheless explores an ancient and
somewhat secret side of East Devon,
which seldom sees much foot traffic.
Nestled in a valley between Colyford and
Seaton, Holyford Woods is one of
Britain's oldest surviving natural
woodlands, and its antiquity is reflected
in the diversity of native flora and fauna
that you may spy on this fantastic foray
around its colourful corners.

Aside from the occasional walker, this
small but historic woodland is populated
by roe deer, badgers, foxes, woodpeckers,
dormice, bats, owls, weasels and wood
mice, as well as countless interesting
insects, butterflies and bees.

This walk starts from the top of Seaton
Down Road, where a picnic spot overlooks
Seaton Bay and offers a reasonably large
(and usually under-used) parking area.
Very carefully cross the A3052, pass
through a gate and walk down a field
with the hedge on your right. After
about 150m you'll reach the entrance to
Holyford Woods, which is accessed via a
kissing gate.

During spring you'll find the footpaths
here fringed by a spellbinding cavalcade
of bluebells, and in autumn the woods are
kaleidoscopically colourful, with leaves of
every shade falling riotously around your
ears. Summer brings dappled light and
long evenings ripe for rambling through
glades made aromatic with wild garlic,
and in winter the holly has its day, while
the denuded trees permit walkers a better
look at the little brook that wends
through these woods on its way to join
the River Axe.

About 100m in, the path forks. Stay left
and walk through an opening where
introduced conifers are slowly being

◀ Entrance to Holyford Woods

cleared to create a view through to Holyford Brook and the marsh, where alder and ever-thirsty willows gather to drink. For most of its length the brook is more accurately described as a goyle, or sunken stream.

Soon after the lower route rejoins the track to your right, the path bears right and crosses a wooden footbridge. You're now entering the older northern half of the woodland, where you'll wander past long-standing oak, ash and birch trees, with holly, hazel and hawthorn thriving beneath their boughs.

After escaping axes and fires for millennia, these woods were almost annihilated in recent years. On the south side, locally known as The Hangings (because of its steepness), the former owners, South West Water, replaced wild-growing furze with conifers, sparking a conservation drive by horrified local walkers. Later, the whole valley was threatened with flooding, as part of a planned reservoir, but it survived and received official protection to become England's 1000th Local Nature Reserve.

The path shadows the brook, before climbing and forking again. The described route goes left, but you can go right to cut the walk short, crossing a footbridge at the bottom of the hill (and then skipping the instructions in the following paragraph).

Take the upper path to ascend to the top of the woods before bearing right and flowing down along a beautiful mixed-woodland trail to a T-junction. Turning left will take you out of the woods towards Colyford, but this route goes right to walk back to the brook and cross it via the footbridge mentioned above.

Follow the path left after the bridge until you meet the main track you walked along earlier, and then retrace your steps to leave the wood, climb through the field and return to the picnic/parking spot on Seaton Down Road.

25

A slice of Lyme

Distance **11.5km** Time **3 hours 30 (one way)**
Terrain **rural footpaths, country lanes,
coastal trail** Map **OS Explorer 116**
Access **Axminster Train Station is well
served by buses and there is parking here;
return by bus (X51, X53) from Lyme Regis
to Axminster Train Station**

Exploring the bucolic borderland
between Devon and Dorset, this walk
leads from the ancient carpet-making
market town of Axminster to the edge of
lovely Lyme Regis, tiptoeing around the
route of the retired railway that once ran
between them. The Axminster to Lyme
Regis rail service might be extinct, but its
fossilised remains are still visible in the
valley, most spectacularly in the form of
the Cannington Viaduct, a mothballed
engineering masterpiece that stands as a
towering tribute to a bygone era. In the
absence of a steam train, you can return
by bus from Lyme Regis to Axminster.

Often called 'the Pearl of the Dorset
Coast', originally Lyme was Devon's jewel.
Historically, the border between
Dumnonia (Devon) and Dornsaete
(Dorset) ran down the River Lim (or Lym),
placing most of Lyme in Devon.

A profitable salt industry existed in
Lyme during mediaeval times and, in
774AD, King Cynewulf (Saxon ruler of
Wessex) gifted a slice of it to the bishop of
Sherborne. The area of Lyme that
remained in royal hands became 'Lyme
Regis', and this valuable piece of surf and
turf is now deemed to be in Dorset.

Start by taking the exit road from
Axminster Train Station. Turn right on
King Edward Road, follow this around a
bend and take another right onto
Musbury Road (A358). Cross, then turn
left onto Woodbury Lane. When this road
forks, stay left (still Woodbury Lane).
Ignore the first footpath going right, but
take the second, just after a collection of

buildings at Chattan.

Follow the path until it meets the busy A35. Carefully cross and continue through fields until the footpath meets a laneway, where you turn left and walk to Trinity Hill Road. Turn right and, after about 250m, hook a left and enter Trinity Woods along a track. Follow the main track through the woods, ignoring turns to the left and right, until you emerge from the trees at Woodhouse Hill.

Take a right onto the road and then shortly afterwards turn left at a T-junction onto Woodhouse Lane. The East Devon Way soon joins you from the right, but continue along it for just a few hundred metres before turning right on Holcombe Lane, which leads to T-junction with Cannington Lane. Turn right and follow this lane until it goes under the impressive Cannington Viaduct.

Just before a house, a gate leads left to a footpath. Take this and climb uphill across the field, bearing right towards a house, where the path meets Horseman's Hill. Follow the lane for a few hundred metres until you come to a footpath going right. Take this to reach Gore Lane, then turn right and walk until you encounter the busy A3052.

Carefully cross and go down Ware Lane directly opposite. When the lane forks, bear left and continue until you see the South West Coast Path signposted off to the right. As you meet the footpath, you're finally leaving Devon and entering Dorset.

Go left on the path and follow it all the way into Lyme Regis where you'll see the Cobb. This 13th-century stone pier, which curls its attractive arm protectively around the western end of the harbour, was the location for one of the most unforgettable scenes in modern cinema when Meryl Streep, looking out to sea in her black cloak, played the enigmatic 'French Lieutenant's Woman' in the 1981 film adaptation of the John Fowles novel.

After exploring the pier and seafront, catch the bus back to Axminster.

◂ Cannington Viaduct

Blackbury Camp to Southleigh

Distance 7.5km **Time** 2 hours 30
Terrain woodland tracks and bridleways,
quiet country lanes, village streets
Map OS Explorer 115 **Access** parking at
Blackbury Camp (free)

This rural ramble links an Iron Age
hillfort with the lovely little hamlet of
Southleigh, nestled in the heart of the
East Devon Hills between Seaton and
Honiton. In spring, Blackbury Camp
famously floods with an incoming tide of
bluebells, while each autumn the scene
is set ablaze with a palette of pastel
colours, the bowl formed by the ancient
fort filling with falling red, orange and
yellow leaves. During summer it's an
idyllic sun-dappled spot for a picnic,
while winter occasionally brings a
smattering of snow to this elevated
corner of the county.

Whatever the weather, the woods around
here are a joy to explore. If you don't fancy
a long walk, it's a great place to quickly
stretch your legs while patrolling the
ramparts, but for a more adventurous
amble, follow this route through the
Southleigh Hills.

Blackbury Camp is owned by English
Heritage, but access is open and free, and
you can park right beside the prehistoric
site. Start with a stroll back in time by
wandering along the defensive walls of the
fort, imagining what life was like here for
tribal people 2400 years ago.

Although it's now completely
surrounded by woods, the fort is perched
upon a hill and would have enjoyed
commanding views when it was built. The
site was excavated in Victorian times and
again in the 1950s, when artefacts
unearthed included an oven, pottery and

◀ Bluebells of Blackbury Camp in bloom

an arsenal of over 1000 slingstones.

The camp's original use isn't fully understood, but archaeologists believe it was occupied for several centuries from around 400BC. The flint-and-clay structure has weathered well, and you can still walk right around the 3m-high ramparts, which form an oval about 200m long by 100m wide. The most unusual element is a triangular barbican by the original entrance on the southern side.

When you've almost circumnavigated the site, turn right and locate a permissive path leading to a wide track which travels downhill through a tunnel formed by oak, birch and chestnut trees. Keep an eye out for deer in these woods.

The track bears left and eventually arcs around to the road. Climb the stile here and turn right along the lane. (Alternatively, for a short walk, you can continue on the track, which leads back to the camp and car park.)

After about 750m, cross the road and turn left onto a footpath, climb over another stile and traverse a field. At the other end, turn right onto a road and then right again onto a broad bridleway that leads along the tree-fringed spine of the

Southleigh Hills. The track crosses a road, continues for several hundred metres and then forks.

Bear right and descend to another road, where you turn left and walk into Southleigh village. Beyond the attractive church there isn't much here, so don't get your hopes up about scoring a cream tea.

Cross the stream and turn left, and then left again to walk up a hill which offers a good view back to the church. After a short distance, take the bridleway leading left up a steep wooded incline. At the junction you passed earlier, turn right and retrace your steps along the track, crossing the first road and turning left on the second. Ignore the stile on your left and continue along the country road, turning right at the T-junction to return to Blackbury Camp.

29

Killerton loop

Distance **5.5km** Time **1 hour 30**
Terrain **woodland tracks, bridleways,
field-hopping footpaths and a small
section of road** Map **OS Explorer 114**
Access **buses (1A, 1B) from Exeter and
Tiverton to Killerton Turn, about 1km
from the start; parking at Killerton Park,
northern end (free)**

**The palatial house and glorious gardens
at Killerton were donated to the National
Trust by Sir Richard Acland, a Labour
MP and passionate believer in public
land ownership who didn't flinch from
following through on his principles
even at the cost of his hereditary home,
a Georgian manor built on an estate
that had been in his family since
the 17th century.**

With that in mind, it would be
a shame not to explore this
wonderful wild arena, which
spills across 2590 hectares of
prime mid-Devon land, a
great green mix of
leafy woodlands,
working farms and manicured lawns,
punctuated by the odd mighty oak tree
and one Iron Age hillfort.

This walk skirts the edge of the
Killerton Estate, following bridleways and
public and permissive footpaths, but amid
a sometimes-knotted tangle of trails, it is
quite easy to accidentally stray directly
onto Trust property where, technically,
non-members are supposed to pay an
entry fee. If you do go wrong and
inadvertently find yourself inside the
estate, you could always cough up on the
way out, or perhaps swap a donation for a
cuppa in the café, but at least you know
Sir Richard wouldn't have been a bit
bothered by your tiny trespass.

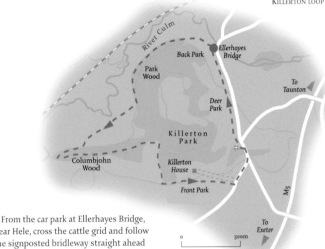

Back Park
Ellerhayes Bridge
Park Wood
River Culm
To Taunton
Deer Park
Killerton Park
Columbjohn Wood
Killerton House
Front Park
M5
To Exeter

0   500m

From the car park at Ellerhayes Bridge, near Hele, cross the cattle grid and follow the signposted bridleway straight ahead towards the woods, through the Back Park, with the River Culm and a railway line off to your right. Ignore the paths leading left up the hill, and stay on the bridleway as it enters Park Wood.

Myriad paths dissect these woods, where you might well see wild deer, but stick to the main track, an old carriage drive, which shadows the serpentine curves of the Culm, a major tributary of the River Exe. Cross a cattle grid and leave the trees, then continue along the bridleway until you go through a gate.

Two paths turn left in quick succession here – you can take either – both climb into Columbjohn Wood, where beech, oak, sycamore and chestnut trees bend in the breeze. If you take the first path, keep right when it forks; if you take the second, it will merge with the first just before you emerge into a clearing called Cross Parks.

Walk across the meadow to the 'Bluebell Gate', but don't go through it; instead turn right and descend the hill, with the hedge and fence on your left.

Turn left through a gate in the hedge and walk though the field adjacent to Killerton House, which sits to your left with its raised garden behind a fence. Follow this public footpath through the Front Park all the way to the road, pass through a gate and turn left to walk past the main entrance to the property.

Stay on the road, being mindful of traffic, as it bears left. A few hundred metres on, a track leads left to the estate chapel. Take this track, and, when it opens up, turn right to stroll down though the Deer Park and the Back Park all the way back to Ellerhayes Bridge.

The evocative appeal of the English Riviera goes well beyond the region's name, which conjures up images of sun-splattered beaches, scenic estuaries, serpentine rivers and cute country villages. In this instance, reality and image marry up most harmoniously, and what you expect is pretty much what you get.

The flipside of this otherwise happy situation is that this small slice of Devon is possibly as popular as all the rest of the county put together, which can make the towns and beaches of Brixham, Paignton and Torquay busy during the summer. However, walkers know how to wander away to the wildest looking headlands and through the thickest woods available. And compact though it may be, Tor Bay still manages to make that possible, several times over. In fact, the Riviera has done such a stellar job of preserving its charm despite its mass appeal that the entire region has been declared a UNESCO Global Geopark – becoming the first 'urban' area ever to be granted the coveted status.

When you run out of new turf to explore in the Riviera, there's the whole cornucopia of the South Hams to discover. This region encompasses the seductive South Devon coast and hinterland sandwiched between southern Dartmoor and the sea, from just below Brixham to the eastern outskirts of Plymouth.

The South Hams is every bit as scenic as the Riviera. Its largely unspoilt shoreline forms most of the South Devon Area of Outstanding Natural Beauty, and it offers a much more raw and remote experience for those seeking walks on the wild side.

Several estuaries cut into this coast, with its numerous historic harbour towns and defensive battlements, as well as ancient and often character-filled pubs.

Amid all this unpolished perfection, there are many softer sheltered spots, too, with gentle sandy beaches and excellent swimming. The diversity of the wildlife is extraordinary, with countless coastal and migratory bird species, as well as seals, dolphins and behemoth basking sharks.

South Hams coastline ▶

South Hams and the Riviera

Yealm Mouth meander

Distance 11.5km **Time** 4 hours
Terrain clifftop tracks, country lanes,
riverside trails and forest footpaths
Map OS Explorer OL20 **Access** bus (94)
from Plymouth and Yealmpton to Noss
Mayo; limited parking in Noss Mayo
car park (free)

This ramble in the realm of the Yealm
starts in the delightful Devon village of
Noss Mayo, which sits on the southern
side of Newton Creek, a tributary of the
main river. From here, woodland trails
and quiet country lanes lead to a section
of the South West Coast Path that
contorts itself around 18 coves before
turning into the Yealm Estuary at
Wembury Bay and leading back to the
hamlet along a riparian route brimming
with charm.

This headland is just south of Plymouth,
and Royal Navy destroyers from Devonport
Naval Base are a common, somewhat
spectral sight as they do drills in the
English Channel. Look out too, for the
bobbing heads of sunbathing seals.

From the corner of the little car park in
Noss Mayo, enter Brooking's Down Wood.
This copse is catacombed with tracks and
trails, but follow the main path and turn
sharp left at the first fork. Skirting the
northeast edge of the woods, take the next
left to exit the trees by a road.

Carefully cross this and pick up another
path, which ascends through more woods
for a few hundred metres before emerging
at a crossroads. Go straight across and
follow the lane to a T-junction, where you
turn left. The road passes Rowden Farm
and continues to Stoke Cross; go straight
over towards Revelstoke Caravan Park.

Pass through the park and bear right,
going past the Saxon-era Church of St
Peter the Poor Fisherman, parts of which
date to 1226. Keep close to the coast as the
path exits the caravan park and slithers
around the curves of umpteen coves,
crossing Netton, Snellings and Gunrow's

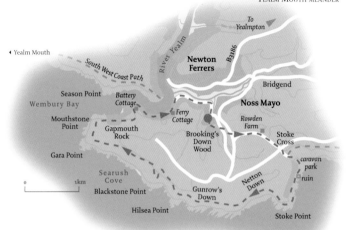

◄ Yealm Mouth

Newton Ferrers

Noss Mayo

To Yealmpton

River Yealm

B3186

Bridgend

South West Coast Path

Season Point

Wembury Bay

Battery Cottage

Ferry Cottage

Rowden Farm

Mouthstone Point

Gapmouth Rock

Brooking's Down Wood

Stoke Cross

Gara Point

caravan park

ruin

Searush Cove

Blackstone Point

Gunrow's Down

Netton Down

Hilsea Point

Stoke Point

0   1km

Downs, and serving up fantastic vistas at every turn.

The well-formed doubletrack along this stretch was built in the 1880s by local landowner Lord Revelstoke (aka Edward Baring, of Barings Bank fame), who wowed visitors by taking them on horse-and-carriage tours of his backyard. Still known as Revelstoke Drive, or sometimes the Nine Mile, it passes an old ruined cottage at a vantage point close to Hilsea Point, where Great Mewstone island looms into view across the waves of Wembury Bay.

Mew is an old word for 'herring gull', and these birds are now the only inhabitants of this isle – once the home of a local man, banished there for several years as punishment for a minor crime. The island dominates your view as the path continues, passing through the gardens of Warren's Cottage, where Lord Revelstoke's guests would take tea, and bounding

through The Warren, which, as the name suggests, was historically a rabbit farm.

As you pass Gara and Mouthstone Points, and round Gapmouth Rock, you enter the embrace of the Yealm Estuary, and a drystone wall appears on your left. The path descends to follow a sheltered and scenic riverside route, going past Battery and then Ferry Cottages, to the Landing Stage, where a sign displays old ferry prices: 1 penny per person (2p on a Sunday), a penny per bag of potatoes, and three pence for each pony or ass. In summer, ferries still run across the Yealm to the west bank, although the fares may have moved north!

Follow the path through Ferry Wood, along the banks of Newton Creek, back to Noss Mayo, where you can enjoy a well-earned bite and beer in the glorious garden of the Ship Inn.

35

Burgh Island hop

Distance **6.5km** Time **3 hours**
Terrain **clifftop tracks, sandy beach,
footpaths through fields, country lanes;
check tide times before you cross the
causeway** Map **OS Explorer OL20**
Access **bus (875) from Plymouth to
Bigbury-on-Sea; parking in Bigbury-on-
Sea (parking charge)**

**The focal point of this walk is Burgh
Island – South Devon's answer to
St Michael's Mount. It might have an
art deco-shaped hotel in place of the
famous Cornish castle and medieval
church, but Burgh boasts bucketloads of
history of its own.**

In its glory days, the hotel hosted the
likes of Noël Coward, Edward and Mrs
Simpson, Winston Churchill and Agatha
Christie – who set two novels here, *And*

Then There Were None and the Hercule
Poirot mystery *Evil Under the Sun*. The
hotel is thought to be built on top of an
ancient monastery, and the entire island
was once a notorious hangout for
smugglers and pirates.

Most people are drawn to the island to
wander the footpaths or have a pint in the
historic Pilchard Inn. If you want to walk
to Burgh Island, however, you'll have to
time your visit to coincide with low tide,
when it's possible to stroll straight across
the sandy causeway. Once the sea has
rolled in, you can still visit via the quirky
sea tractor (but always double check
return times).

You don't have to set foot on the island
to appreciate the view, though, and this is
a great walk all year round, even if you
miss the tides and the aqua tractor isn't

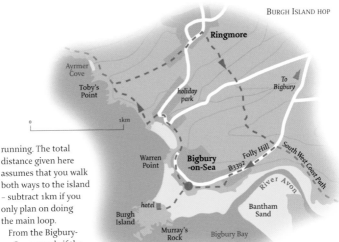

running. The total distance given here assumes that you walk both ways to the island – subtract 1km if you only plan on doing the main loop.

From the Bigbury-on-Sea car park, if the tide is out and you wish to explore the island, head straight across the beach and causeway. Once back on the mainland, follow the coast path signs along a section of road leading west out of town and up a hill until a footpath branches left.

The path arcs around the shoreline to Challaborough Bay, which is essentially a giant holiday park facing onto a broad sandy beach. You can wander along the sand, paddle through the surf or stick to the South West Coast Path, which sneaks through the park until you reach the base of the headland opposite.

The trail continues to hug the seaside as you climb this grassy rise. At the top, a path breaks right, leading inland over the brow of the hill, across fields and along a clear track until you reach Ringmore. Ignore the first right turn and walk through the village, taking the second

right – a little lane, which soon segues into a footpath.

Stick to this path as it leads you on a little rollercoaster ride, through a copse of trees, down a hillside to a stream and then back up another climb. Passing through several gates, carefully cross the road and then pick up the path again as it drops and then rises once more before delivering you to Folly Hill (the B3392).

Hang a right here, and follow the footpath on the inside of the hedge (to avoid walking on the road) until you're forced to cross the tarmac, where another path leads down to Sharpland Point and the mouth of the Avon River.

Bigbury Bay is a popular South Devon surf spot, and you'll likely spot kayakers and board riders catching breaks as you shadow the shore back to the car park.

Bolt Head

Distance 8.5km **Time** 3 hours
Terrain cliff-top paths and secret beaches
Map OS Explorer OL20 **Access** parking in
the National Trust car park at East Soar
(free); nearby Marlborough and
Salcombe are served by bus (X606)
from Kingsbridge

A cracking clifftop crawl, which hugs the
headlands and sidles alongside a
shoreline accessible only on foot, around
Bolt Head to Starehole Bay and the beach
at South Sands, just outside Salcombe.
The route rambles back via a mysterious
mansion – once home to an eccentric
inventor – and a surprise walker-friendly
tearoom housed in a barn.

From the car park, ignore the track
going down to East Soar Farm, and
instead walk south on the continuation
of the laneway you drove up to get here.
After about 100m, take the footpath

going right and stroll across farmland
towards the sea, passing buildings at
Middle Soar. Continue to a T-junction just
above The Warren, turn left and follow the
trail until it meets the South West Coast
Path (SWCP).

Follow the SWCP as it wends through
dramatic wind-sculpted rocks and rounds
beautiful Bolt Head. Keep your eyes
peeled for peregrine falcons, kestrels, cirl
buntings and rare Dartford warblers here,
and enjoy the stunning views across the
Mew Stone rock formations and out
across the restless waves – which cover a
multitude of wrecks.

This coast is as dangerous as it is
delightful. One infamous incident in 1760
saw *HMS Ramillies* flounder near Bolt Tail
– a tragedy so terrible that local folk
songs still lament the loss of over 700
lives. Bits of the boat apparently adorn
local houses, and divers explore the

remains, which now haunt a flooded cave below the cliff.

The path skirts Starehole Bay, location of a secret beach and another wreck – the *Herzogin Cecilie*, a four-masted steel barque better known as *The Duchess*, which won the Grain Race from Australia eight times before coming to grief on the rocks here in 1937. Her submerged skeleton is sometimes visible from the clifftop.

When the track splits at Starehole Bottom, take the lower option (right) and pass beneath Sharp Tor. Kingsbridge Estuary yawns before you, busy with little fishing boats, yachts, kayaks, ribs and ferries full of tourists.

Keep following the coastal path past the gloriously named Stink Cove and Splatcove Point towards South Sands, which boasts a fancy hotel and fantastic Bo's Beach Café, where you can grab a coffee, a pizza or hire a kayak.

Retrace your steps back up the hill, but then veer right and walk past the National Trust property of Overbeck's – former home of scientist Otto Overbeck, a pioneer of electrotherapy and inventor of the dubious sounding 'Rejuvenator', who also cultivated the still-thriving tropical plants in the gardens.

Go around the property, take the

first left to cut across Fir Wood, and continue to the top of Sharp Tor to enjoy magnificent views across to Prawle Point – Devon's most southerly piece of terra firma.

Follow the footpath around the cliffs, then look for a fingerpost sign pointing towards the East Soar Outdoor Experience, where you can visit the wonderful Walkers' Hut. Hot and cold drinks are available here, along with homemade cakes and other treats, either served by the friendly owners or left out for you to help yourself, with an honesty box provided for payment. A small playground and a hobby farm keep little walkers happy.

When you're done, wander on through the farm and follow the track all the way back to the car park, passing a small airstrip on your right.

◄ Above the cliffs of Bolt Head

Prawle Point prowl

**Distance 4.5km Time 3 hours
Terrain coastal and clifftop trails,
woodland paths, quiet country lanes
Map OS Explorer OL20 Access parking
in East Prawle village**

There's a distinctly bacon-flavoured
theme going on along this stretch of the
South Hams coast – with names such as
the Pig's Nose, Ham Stone and Gammon
Head all featuring loud and proud on the
map – and this short but challenging trot
will put a smile on all walkers' chops,
with secret beaches and lovely lookouts
over Lannacombe Bay.

Pull up in East Prawle and park by the
village green, just across from the local
pub, the Pig's Nose – a 500-year-old
former smugglers' drinking den, which is
still renowned as a buzzing little local
alehouse, with a crackling atmosphere.

Walk out of the village, passing the pub

on your right, and following the road
around to the left (west), to go past the
buildings of Higher Farm. Keep following
the lane until you meet a Y-junction,
where you take the bridleway leading left.

Follow this rocky, rubbly route as it
begins to open up with views through the
valley and out to sea. At a junction, the
bridleway shoots off left, but keep going
straight on, through a gate, following the
footpath as it hugs the left flank of the
combe. Ahead, to your right, the Pig's Nose
and Ham Stone wallow in the waters just
beyond the Kingsbridge Estuary.

The path descends through steep fields,
and when it finally hits the shore you will
see Gammon Head immediately to your
right. Directly below – hidden completely
until you're right above it – is a
sensational sandy beach, secretly tucked
into the nape of the cove. Access to both
the headland and the bay is possible, but

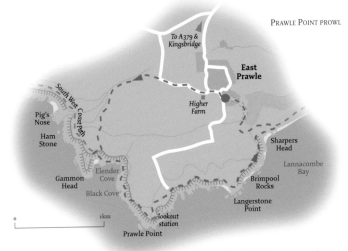

To A379 &
Kingsbridge

**East
Prawle**

South West Coast path

Pig's
Nose

Ham
Stone

*Higher
Farm*

Sharpers
Head

Lannacombe
Bay

Gammon
Head

Elender
Cove

Black Cove

Brimpool
Rocks

Langerstone
Point

*lookout
station*

Prawle Point

0   1km

a bit dicey in places. Be particularly careful on the rocks around the headland if it's wet, when conditions are super slippery and the drops dramatic and deadly.

Once you've had your fill of Gammon Head, turn the other cheek and continue along the coast in the opposite direction, following the path west as it skirts the cliff tops of Elender and Black Cove. Trace the contours of the cliffs until you reach Prawle Point, the most southerly part of mainland Devon.

For all the porcine wordplay around here, the name 'Prawle' dates back to an Anglo-Saxon word *Prawhyll*, meaning 'lookout'. And, right enough, there is a Lookout Station here, manned by vigilant volunteers, who are usually happy to welcome you in to check out their fantastic view across the channel. The little building next door has lots of good info about local history and wildlife (from birds to basking sharks), and a fascinating

infographic detailing the many wrecks that litter the wild ocean floor here.

This seemingly quiet spot has an action-packed past. The people of Prawle witnessed the Spanish Armada sailing past in 1588, and the Battle of Prawle Point took place here in 1793, during the Napoleonic Wars with France. In 1815, Napoleon himself was held on a ship just off Prawle Point for several days, awaiting exile to St Helena.

Descend the hill and follow the coast around Lannacombe Bay which contains some fabulously named features, including Stinking Cove and Ballsaddle Rock away to the northeast. At Sharpers Head, go left along a clearly signposted path, which leads all the way back to East Prawle. On the way, a small shortcut breaks right and takes you through a very steep field. It's a stern climb, but there's no better way to earn your beer when you get back to the Pig's Nose.

◄ Gammon Head

Dartmouth's coast and castles

Distance **6.5km** Time **2 hours**
Terrain **coastal trails, hilltop tracks,
woodland paths and quiet country lanes**
Map OS Explorer OL20 Access **bus (3) from
Kingsbridge and (X64) from Totnes to
Dartmouth; parking in Little Dartmouth
National Trust car park (donation)**

**Attack Dartmouth Castle the healthy,
stealthy way – by marching there. This
walk tiptoes along a series of sneaky
cross-country trails, which link to form
a scenic inland route to the 15th-century
castle from Little Dartmouth, going via
the ruined remains of a less well-known
Civil War fort, perched above the
battlements. After breaching these
historic defences, loop back at a leisurely
pace, exploring the South West Coast
Path, complete with coves commonly
populated by curious seals.**

From the small National Trust car park
in Little Dartmouth, take a right and head
along Castle Road, a lane leading east.

Follow signage for the Diamond Jubilee
Way, a 6km loop (different to the one
you're currently following), which was
designated in 2012.

Shortly after passing some buildings,
the lane skirts around the flanks of a hill,
offering views across the Dart Estuary.
About 1km on, you'll pass another
building on your right and just after this a
smaller path leads left into the trees. Take
this and climb along twisty tree-fringed
trails to Gallants Bower, the lofty location
of a fort built to defend Dartmouth
against Parliamentarian forces during the
English Civil War.

The Roundheads gave the Royalists a
proper pasting here in 1646, and the fort
was later destroyed, but what it lacks in
physical remains the site more than
makes up for with fantastic 360-degree
views of the estuary, city, coastline,
harbour and hinterland.
On a clear day, you can
easily make out the

Kingswear

To Dartmouth

One Gun Point

Warfleet

Gallants Bower

castle   castle

Mill Bay Cove

Sugary Cove

B3205

Deadman's Cove

Ladies Cove

Blackstone Point

Castle Road

Compass Cove

South West Coast Path

Little Dartmouth

To Stoke Fleming

Willow Cove

Meg Rocks

Combe Point

Redlap Cove

Warren Point

Dancing Beggars

0   1km

Daymark above Kingswear on the far headland, a beacon built in 1864 to assist shipping.

Descend from the summit and pick up the main path, which drops straight into the area dominated by St Petroc's Church and the castle. At the behest of Edward III, who was concerned about French attacks, the original fortalice was built in 1388 by wealthy local merchant and privateer (or pirate, depending on your opinion) John Hawley, who was Dartmouth's mayor and the inspiration for the colourful character of the shipman in Geoffrey Chaucer's *The Canterbury Tales*.

The 'new' castle was completed above Warfleet Creek in 1494. On the opposite bank you can clearly see Kingswear Castle, constructed at the beginning of the 16th century to help defend Dartmouth. If the harbour was threatened, a chain could be drawn across the river, to prevent enemy shipping entering the estuary; any that slipped through could be sunk by heavy fire from Dartmouth's dedicated Gun Tower. The area has a military tradition that predates the castle by several centuries – boats left from here in 1145, full of knights on their way to fight in the Second Crusade. These days a more peaceful scene prevails, and directly below the castellated stonework seals are often seen in Castle Cove. The whole site is operated by English Heritage, and can be explored during standard opening hours.

Before heading back, you can drop down to Sugary Cove to enjoy some sweet beach action on a broad arc of sand. Otherwise, pick up the South West Coast Path and follow it around Deadman's and Ladies Coves to Blackstone Point, where the estuary views are again sublime.

Keep following the coast path to Warren Point, opposite the Dancing Beggar rocks, where it turns inland and helpfully delivers you straight back to your car.

◄ Dartmouth Castle with Kingswear Castle beyond

Kingswear to Coleton Fishacre

Distance 9.5km Time 3 hours 30
Terrain river and coastal trails, woodland
tracks and country lanes
Map OS Explorer OL20 Access bus (120)
from Paignton to Kingswear or travel to
Dartmouth and take the ferry to
Kingswear; limited parking in Kingswear

Historic Kingswear hums with an excited
buzz during summer, when the pretty
little town is perpetually full of families
out for a jaunt on the steam trains that
run along the riverfront. But, even at the
height of the season, you'll soon leave
the madding crowd behind on the trails
that head south around the river mouth
to explore the coves and cliffs of the
South Devon coast and all the way round
to the Arts-and-Crafts-style country pile
at Coleton Fishacre.

During the Second World War,
Kingswear was a base for the Free French

Navy, which ran rescue missions across
the channel, supplying munitions to the
Resistance and returning with wounded
fighters. Ferries have been transporting
people to and fro across the river here
since at least 1365, and right into the 20th
century Kingswear remained the doorway
to Dartmouth for visitors from London
and Exeter, who arrived on the Great
Western Railway, and then boarded boats.

Whether you arrive by ferry or car, leave
the marina, walk along Beacon Road and
hang a left at Alma Steps, which climb to
Beacon Lane. Turn right at the top and
follow the sealed surface into the trees,
where it becomes Castle Road. Keep
going, past a couple of buildings, until the
lane bends left.

To your right, down at water level, are
the remains of Gommerock. In the 15th
century, a huge chain extended across the
river from here to the original Dartmouth

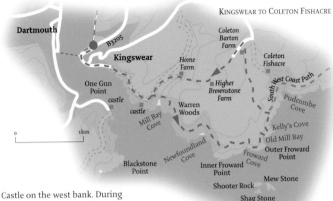

Castle on the west bank. During an attack, the chain could be drawn tight to prevent enemy ships entering the estuary. Kingswear Castle also erupts out of the river here. Completed in 1502, this fortification was built to assist the new Dartmouth Castle (visible opposite) in its defensive duties.

Follow the road around the elbow, then take the wooden steps leading right, steeply descending into Mill Bay Cove. On the opposite side of this small combe, more steps ascend through Warren Woods. The South West Coast Path clambers up onto the clifftops here and offers spectacular views as it wends around Newfoundland Cove and Froward Points, with Shooter Rock, Shag Stone and Mew Stone protruding proudly from the ocean waves to your right.

At Inner Froward Point you'll see the National Trust-owned remains of a lookout hut and Brownstone Battery, a large gun emplacement which was built during the early years of the Second World War to defend Dartmouth against the threat of German attack. It is worth exploring the information centre before you continue.

Keep right when the path forks and follow the main coast track, which descends to Old Mill Bay. Go past Kelly's Cove and continue towards Pudcombe Cove until, just after crossing a small stream, you take a permissive path that turns left to head inland, skirting around the National Trust's Coleton Fishacre property – former home of the D'Oyly Carte family, who made their name and fortune through a theatre company, staging Gilbert and Sullivan operas.

The path climbs to Coleton Barton Farm, where you turn left along a lane to Higher Brownstone. Ignore the path leading left towards the beacon, battery and coast, and continue straight on along a track that ascends towards Pinewoods. At Home Farm, follow the track as it bears left to pass the steps you took earlier down to Mill Bay Cove. Ignore these and retrace your steps into Kingswear.

◄ Kingswear Castle and the Dart Estuary

Dittisham and the Dart Valley

**Distance 8km Time 2 hours 30
Terrain quiet country lanes,
woodland paths and creekside trails
Map OS Explorer OL20 Access ferry from
Greenway to Dittisham; parking in The
Level car park (free), Lower Dittisham
(not the more obvious riverside car park)**

From the charming riverside village of
Dittisham, this route rambles across one
of the finest dales in Devon, serving up
sensational views along the Dart Valley
as walkers follow the flow of the water,
across magical meadows and through
wonderful woodlands.

The walk traces a section of the Dart
Valley Trail, a 27km, day-long epic hiking
adventure that links Totnes and
Dartmouth. It crosses land owned by the
descendants of Sir Walter Raleigh, who
spent time in Greenway on the far bank

and embarked on many a character-
building foray into the forests and fields
this side of the Dart during his youth.

From the small car park in Lower
Dittisham (The Level), turn left and walk
in the direction of the quay where
ferries depart for Greenway. As the
road bends left to the right of the white
house, however, pick up the lane that
leads up the hill to the River Farm,
turning right at a fingerpost just before
you reach the farm itself.

Take the next left and climb steeply up
Glebe Plantation. Be sure to stop here and
take in the views across Dittisham and
along the valley, which is a kaleidoscope
of colour in autumn but a beautiful sight
to behold at any time of year.

The footpath meets a road, where you
turn left and walk for about 100m before
breaking left again, onto a signposted

◄ Dittisham and the River Dart

Dart Valley Trail

■ *Ferry Cottage*

Dittisham

Cott Farm ■

The River Farm

Glebe Plantation

Fire Beacon Hill

High Bosomzeale Farm

Bosomzeal

Higher Noss Point

River Dart

Rough Hole Point

0   1km

Dart Valley Trail

Old Mill Creek

Dartmouth

permissive path that leads across Fire Beacon Hill. This site, near Bosomzeal, features a 3m-high mound, built in the 16th century on the crest of a high spur overlooking the Dart Estuary, on top of which warning fires were lit in the event of enemy ships being spotted in the channel. This very beacon would have been ablaze in 1588 as the Spanish Armada approached the English coast, disturbing Sir Francis Drake's game of bowls in nearby Plymouth.

Follow this path until it meets a lane, where you turn left. Look out for a signposted right turn after about 200m; take this and follow the path as it leads downhill, across several fields and through a couple of gates, before bearing left into a copse. Stick to the main path

here, ignoring the numerous tracks that lead into the woods, and continue towards Old Mill Creek, which you should be able to hear even if you can't see it through the trees.

The path continues to shadow the creek until you meet back up with the Dart Valley Trail. Turn right, and walk uphill along the wide, rubbly bridleway. When this track forks, take the right-hand option and ascend the hill back to Bosomzeal and then Fire Beacon Hill, where you turned off earlier. Ignore this first turn and take the second on your right to retrace your steps down the slope of Glebe Plantation to the car park.

Guns of Brixham

Distance 7km **Time** 3 hours
Terrain coastal trails, woodland tracks,
foreshore footpaths and town pavements
Map OS Explorer OL20 **Access** Brixham is
well served by buses from Paignton,
Torquay and Newton Abbot; parking in
Berry Head car park (parking charge)

A route for walkers who like hikes with
a historical backdrop, this salty stroll
strides through time, each corner
revealing a clue to the many military and
maritime milestones that have taken
place around Brixham, a naval
stronghold since the days of Henry VIII.
The town's history dates back further
still, to Viking times, and a replica of Sir
Francis Drake's globetrotting *Golden Hind*
sits in the harbour – a tribute to the
swashbuckling, bowls-playing, Spaniard-
scaring Englishman, who orchestrated
the defeat of the Armada in 1588.

Brixham is where the Dutch prince
William of Orange landed on 5 November
1688, on his way to becoming King
William III of Great Britain and Ireland
during the Glorious Revolution. In 1944,
thousands of American servicemen left
from here for the D-Day landings, part of
Operation Overlord.

Plenty of action took place between
those dates, as this walk immediately
reveals, with a loop of Berry Head, now a
National Nature Reserve, which led a
former life as a military post, when it was
armed to the teeth with big guns and
tasked with defending the harbour during
the American War of Independence and in
Napoleonic squabbles.

From Berry Head car park, set off with
the sea on your right and head straight
for the entrance to the semi-castellated
walls of Berry Head, which is open and
free year round. The site is well worth
exploring, with features including a
sentry box dating to 1802 and an eccentric
lighthouse – simultaneously the
country's shortest (by stature) and

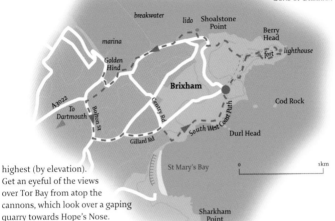

highest (by elevation). Get an eyeful of the views over Tor Bay from atop the cannons, which look over a gaping quarry towards Hope's Nose.

Leaving the fortification the same way you came in, bear right and trace the tree-lined South West Coast Path as it threads through a small woodland and drops towards town. The path joins Berry Head Road, then quickly leaves it again to shimmy past Shoalstone Outdoor Pool, an impressive seawater lido, open in warmer months.

Your approach to town is dominated by the breakwater. It's worth walking to the lighthouse at the far end for the views back on the colourful hill-hugging houses of Brixham – former fishermen's homes – but be aware this will add almost 2km to the walk.

The marina features memorials to the local lifeboat station, one of the world's most decorated, which was set up after a terrible storm destroyed 50 boats and stole more than 100 souls in January 1866. Boats of all descriptions bob in the harbour – once one of Britain's biggest fishing ports – but the most famous, moored next to the statue of King Billy, is the replica of the *Golden Hind*, the galleon that Drake took around the world in 1577–1580, completing the second ever circumnavigation of the planet.

Various routes lead through town – the one marked is easy to follow, going along Fore Street shopping strip, taking the first major left to climb Bolton Street and then breaking left again along Rea Barn Road. Keep right when the street forks around Astley Park sports ground. Shortly afterwards, Rea Barn Road becomes Gillard Road, which segues into a single-track lane at the junction with Centry Road. Here, take the footpath to the right, which leads to the South West Coast Path. Turn left and walk past Durl Head, back to the car park.

◀ A gun at Berry Head fort

Broadsands to Greenway

Distance **12.5km** Time **4 hours**
Terrain **coastal trails, woodland tracks,
foreshore footpaths and town pavements**
Map **OS Explorer OL20** Access **bus (12)
from Newton Abbot, Torquay, Paignton
and Brixham to Broadsands; parking in
Broadsands car park (parking charge)**

**Kicking off beside the brilliant beach in
Broadsands, this mixed-terrain trek
traverses the neck of the Kingswear and
Brixham peninsula to link the coast of
the English Riviera with the riparian face
of the South Hams, seen through the
grounds of Greenway House – once home
to the *grande dame* of murder and mystery,
Agatha Christie.**

At 12.5km, this walk is a challenge, but
it's far from murder and there's no
mystery about what makes it such a killer
choice, with the route using tasty trails to
splice together stunning vistas and
historic houses.

From Broadsands car park, set off east
along the South West Coast Path, with the
white horses of Tor Bay rearing on your
left. Scoot around Churston Point and
Elberry Cove, then head towards
Fishcombe Point. At a junction just before
Brixham Holiday Park, turn right onto the
John Musgrave Heritage Trail, a 56km
long-distance path named after a leading
local rambler. Take note of the boot-
printed arrow trail markers, which you'll
follow all the way to Higher Greenway.

Take the trail to Bascombe Road, where
it does a dogleg and hops over the old
railway. Carefully cross the A3022 at
Churston Cross, pass Alston Farm, where
the lane becomes a path, and climb the
hill to cross the A379. Descend through a
field, taking a right at the bottom.

The Greenway Walk joins you here,
coming in from the right along Combe
Lane, but you should continue straight on
until you reach Higher Greenway Farm,
where the Dart Valley Trail enters from
your left. Continue to a road and turn left;
look left to try and spot a puffing loco
travelling along the Paignton and

Tor Bay

Broadsands

Churston Point

Fishcombe Point

◀ Bust of Agatha Christie

South West Coast Path

Galmpton Warborough Common

Galmpton

A3022

Lower Point

Galmpton Creek

Old Mill Farm

Churston Cross

A3022

Paignton & Dartmouth Railway

JMH Trail

Lower Greenway Farm

A379

Alston Farm

Greenway House

hostel

Higher Greenway Farm

Lupton Park

River Dart

0   2km

Dartmouth Steam Railway, which emerges from a tunnel beneath you.

Pass a youth hostel on your left and go through a gate onto a green track with great views over the River Dart. You're now above Greenway House – a National Trust-owned estate dating to Tudor times, which boasted plenty of interesting backstories even before Agatha Christie moved in and began dumping fictitious murder victims in the boathouse (read *Dead Man's Folly*). It was originally home to Sir Humphrey Gilbert, Newfoundland explorer and half-brother to Sir Walter Raleigh.

Turn right through a gate into the estate. Bear left to explore the house or stick to the right and follow signs for Galmpton to continue the route. Pass through woods to reach Greenway Road, turn right and then enter Lower

Greenway Farm via a stile and footpath on the left. You're on the Greenway Walk now, which traces the riverbank along Kiln Road to Old Mill Farm and the Quays at Galmpton Creek. Continue to a T-junction and take a right on Stoke Gabriel Road towards Galmpton.

At a crossroads, turn left onto Slade Lane and follow this to the great green Galmpton Warborough Common, a historic space used for defensive purposes since Viking times and where, in 1588, Sir John Gilbert of Greenway gathered a 1000-man militia in preparation to repel an impending Spanish invasion. Head – via the old windmill – to the war memorial (a cross) and carefully walk over the A3022.

On the other side, turn right onto Bascombe Road and then look for a footpath leading left. Take this to Broadsands Road, where you turn right, passing under the railway and following the road to the car park.

Hope's Nose

Distance 8km **Time** 3 hours
Terrain coastal trails, headland paths,
woodland tracks and minimal road
walking **Map** OS Explorer OL44
Access Torquay is well served by trains
and buses; parking in Meadfoot Beach car
park (parking charge)

A mecca for sea anglers, Hope's Nose is
a quirky, perky protrusion into Tor Bay.
The limestone peninsula was formed
when England was located in the tropics,
and fascinating fossils can be found
here. Unless you score a particularly
spectacular summer's afternoon, it rarely
feels tropical these days, but it does
offer walkers a wind-blown slice of wild
heaven and some delightful respite
from the bustle of Torquay.

This circular meander clings limpet-like
to the coast, leaving the South West Coast
Path briefly to explore the exposed tip of
the Nose, and tracing a trail also known
as Bishop's Walk, named after the
Victorian-era rambling rector, Henry
Phillpotts, Lord Bishop of Exeter. The
described route turns the other cheek at
Devil's Point and returns via the woods
that cluster around Lincombe Slopes,
passing Kent's Cavern, a cave system once
occupied by our ancient ancestors, where
the oldest evidence of human habitation
in England has been discovered.

Start at Torquay's Meadfoot Beach car
park and walk to its eastern end, where
you'll see a pathway leading down towards
Meadfoot Beach, with its unusual arc of
modern multistorey beach huts. Continue
along the seafront and, when the road
turns left to cut off the Nose, you will see
a footpath leading uphill. Take this path,
climb to the clifftop road, turn right and
then, just past Kilmorie, go right along a
footpath that leads to Thatcher Point.

From this exposed spot there are great
views out over Thatcher Rock, a dramatic
sea stack that boasts an unusual raised
beach, created during the last ice age
when the English Channel was being
born. The rock is now home to noisy

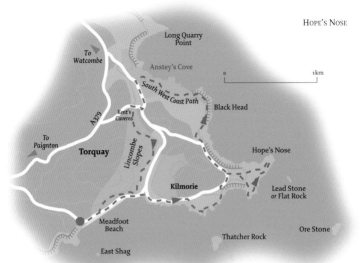

populations of kittiwake and guillemot.

After ambling around this arc, rejoin the road again briefly, turning right and then right again to follow another footpath leading to the tip of Hope's Nose. Rudimentary little tracks allow you to explore the full extent of the proud snout, before leading back to the road.

Turn right, carefully cross the road and pick up a pedestrian pathway that runs parallel to the tarmac. When this path offers you another chance to turn right, take it, cross the road again and follow a pathway that leads behind some houses. This brings you out onto a great section of the South West Coast Path/Bishop's Walk, which continues right around to Black Head and beyond, offering teasing glimpses of Long Quarry Point through the trees.

When you reach Anstey's Cove, turn left into the car park, cross the road and bear left through the green. At the junction of the main road, go right and follow signs to Kents Cavern. These extensive caves (now run as a commercial visitor attraction) were once home to the very earliest humans known to live in North West Europe, and people have been fascinated with them for centuries – an early graffiti artist, William Petre, left his tag on a stalagmite in 1571. Along with ancient human remains, the bones of animals that include sabre tooth tigers, bears, cave lions and mammoths have been found here.

No such mega fauna stalks the woods now, so you can walk without fear through the tree-lined path that skirts the contours of Lincombe Slopes, all the way back to the hillside hotel opposite the car park where your walk began.

◀ Thatcher Rock

Maidencombe and the Valley of Rocks

Distance 5.5km **Time** 1 hour 30
Terrain woodland tracks, coastal trails,
quiet lanes and field-hopping footpaths
Map OS Explorer OL44 **Access** bus (34)
from Torquay to Watcombe; parking in
Watcombe car park (free)

Awaken your inner combe raider on this
short but dramatic dawdle, which starts
at Watcombe and descends into the
surreally red surrounds of the Valley of
Rocks, passing through a landscape laid
down when England was hovering
around the equator some 280 million
years ago. Shadowing the shore, it then
meanders to Maidencombe, where a
secluded beach awaits – along with a
great country pub and the mysterious
Judas Tree – before looping back on a
rural route that captured the heart of
engineer Isambard Kingdom Brunel, who
moved here in the mid-19th century.

The walk covers sections of the
well-marked John Musgrave

Heritage Trail, a 56km long-distance
path dedicated to a local rambler, and
offers bird-spotting hikers sightings of
the endangered cirl bunting. Keep an eye
on the sea too – dolphins and other
marine animals are often glimpsed
along this coast.

From Watcombe car park, ignore signs
leading directly down to the beach
(a continuation of the tight rural lane to
the car park) and instead enter the woods
via a footpath that quickly plunges you
into the Valley of Rocks. Suddenly you
will be in a glorious glade, tinted red by
the clay cliffs that tower to the left.
Unsurprisingly, this area once supported
a thriving terracotta pottery business.

The South West Coast Path meets your
track in the middle of the valley. Go
straight on, ignoring the subsequent left
turn for the John Musgrave Heritage Trail,
and continue to the clifftops. As views of
Babbacombe Bay open up in front, the
path bears left.

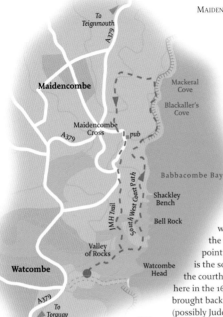

climb over a stile and take the path leading left across the open hillside, with great views back towards Watcombe Head.

At Maidencombe Cross, take a left and follow the lane down to the Thatched Tavern. Nearby, Orestone Manor was the home of Victorian artist J C Horsley, who is credited with inventing the concept of the Christmas card. Another point of interest in Maidencombe is the so-called Judas Tree outside the courthouse, which was planted here in the 16th century after being brought back from the Holy Land (possibly Judea) as a sapling. Theories about its name include the gory story that Judas Iscariot hanged himself from a similar tree.

The bar-room historians in the Thatched Tavern will have an opinion on it, but if you can resist the open invite of the pub, bear slightly right here (instead of going towards the beach and the junction you passed earlier) and follow the road until you see the John Musgrave Heritage Trail forking off to the left.

Follow the Heritage Trail directional arrows along footpaths until you reach the junction you ignored earlier. Turn right here to pass back through the Valley of Rocks to the car park.

Keep following the coast. The path goes past a stile on your left, leading into a farmer's field, but don't cross it – continue on the path that borders the field. Go past Bell Rock and Shackley Bench to reach Maidencombe. A path leads right to the beach, where a shack sells ice creams and drinks during the warmer months.

Keep following the South West Coast Path north, past Blackaller's Cove. At Mackerel Cove, take a left along a clearly marked path heading uphill and inland. About 200m before you hit the A379,

◀ The Thatched Tavern

Dartmoor is where Devon gets serious.
The gentle sea breeze and cream teas
of the county's coastline seem a long
way off when you take on a tor-top walk
and encounter a prehistoric stone circle
or megalith in the midst of the moor.

This is an ancient place, haunted by
mysterious myths and half-known
stories, where clues to what life was like
in ancient Britain lie strewn across an
untamed landscape that has beguiled
mankind for millennia.

You will find real raw beauty on
Dartmoor. Walkers come from all around
the world to explore its tors, experience
its historic villages and pubs, and amble
amid the gorse bushes and woodlands

that cluster around its many restless
rivers, including the Dart, the Bovey,
the Plym, the Teign and the Taw – all of
which will be introduced to you in the
following pages.

Dartmoor offers wild, unadulterated
adventure to those who seek such
thrills, but it doesn't suffer fools gladly.
You should be prepared for any
eventuality with weather conditions,
particularly on the more exposed parts,
and be aware that paths can sometimes
be tricky to follow on the open moor.
But this evocative expanse of wilderness
is a national treasure, which only reveals
its best-kept secrets to those willing
to walk.

Haytor ▶

Dartmoor

Plym Bridge

Distance 8km **Time** 2 hours
Terrain woodland trails, riverside paths,
shared-use rail trail (cycling and walking)
Map OS Explorer OL20 **Access** parking in
Plym Bridge National Trust car park (free)

**Hugging the Plym for its duration,
this walk is a first-class return trip along
the old route of the Great Western
Railway, which skirts the serpentine
riverbanks on the way out and comes
back along a beautiful rail trail that
crosses a trio of viaducts – each one an
engineering masterpiece.**

It's hard to comprehend just how close
you are to Plymouth here – the city seems
very distant as you wend through the
woods and along a wonderful waterway –
a section of the West Devon Way.

From the car park at Plym Bridge, cross
the road and go through a gate to pick up

a beautiful section of path that threads a
piece of land scenically caught between
the river and a long-retired canal.

Ignore a turning off to the right and,
after about 1km, the first of the viaducts
looms large in front of you. Walk under
this impressive bridge and on the other
side you will be met by a clearing in an
old quarry, which is a well-known haunt
of peregrine falcons. Look behind you and
you will doubtless discover several long-
range lenses pointing at you from a hide
on the bridge – the paparazzi of the
twitching world.

Ascend the steps to the viaduct and
turn right to cross the bridge. This is all
part of the rail trail, so mind out for bikes.
Say hello to the birders and, about 100m
after leaving the bridge, look out for some
ill-defined steps leading down to the
banks of the Plym. Take these, then turn

◄ Plym Woods

left and enjoy walking along a sublime stretch of riverside trail.

This continues in glorious fashion for about 2.5km until, at a junction before Bickleigh Bridge, you have to take the track left (the riverside path does continue for a hundred metres or so, but then you hit private property).

As you leave the river, the path ascends steeply. Just before you meet the road, you will encounter the rail trail again – turn left and stride back along this nicely constructed route, enjoying your elevated position among the trees in the Plym Valley. Each viaduct you cross offers views across the river. Trains haven't run along this route for 45 years, but they must have been an awesome sight, steaming through the valley and crossing bridge after bridge.

Cross two of these bridges and just before the third (the one you crossed earlier) take the trail to the right (labelled

as a blue trail) and drop back down to the river. Walk along another sweet section of serpentine path for 1km, before crossing the river at Plym Bridge and returning to the car park.

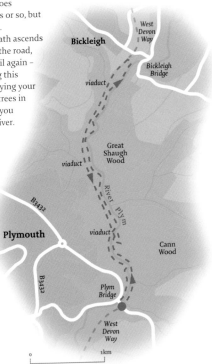

Trowlesworthy Tor

Distance **10km** Time **3 hours**
Terrain **wild open moor, tor tops, tracks**
Map **OS Explorer OL20** Access **parking in
Trowlesworthy Burrows car park, near
Cadover Bridge (free)**

This is a wander on the wild side of
Dartmoor for confident walkers who are
comfortable leaving the beaten path
behind to do some off-piste adventuring,
following line-of-sight navigation across
open moorland. The weather can be as
testing as the terrain, so it is best left for
a fine day – even then come prepared
with extra layers and waterproofs just in
case. Explorers are richly rewarded with
glorious views across a life-affirming
landscape and the chance to discover
ancient stone circles and the remains of
ruined settlements built by Dartmoor
dwellers several thousand years ago.

Cadover Bridge is on a minor road
which heads northwards from Plympton
towards Meavy and Yelverton. Just south
of the bridge, turn onto the track leading
into Brisworthy Burrows, where the still-
young River Plym meanders across

meadows. Park up and set off along the
banks of the river, walking against the
direction of water flow.

Cross Blacka Brook via a small bridge
and follow the track uphill, away from the
river (which is on your left). Follow a
right-hand bend and, within a few
hundred metres, you'll reach
Trowlesworthy Warren House. Skirt
around the buildings and pick up a
distinct path that leads through the
lumpy remains of the historic warren.
Rabbits were introduced to Britain by the
Normans after 1066, and Trowlesworthy
is believed to be the oldest warren on
Dartmoor, possibly dating as far back as
the 13th century.

When you reach a creek, cross the
rudimentary footbridge, turn right and

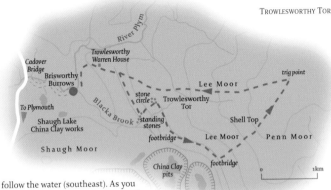

follow the water (southeast). As you walk, Trowlesworthy Tor will tower above, to your left. You'll pass several more basic footbridges, but keep the creek on your right. Out of nowhere you will come across an avenue of astonishing standing stones, which date to 2500–1500BC. Follow these up the hill to an impressive stone circle.

Continue up the hill a little way, until you meet a large loaf-shaped rock. Look to your right here and you will see a row of stones and a fence – walk to this, crossing a stream, and pick up a path following the contour of the hill. To your right you will see the vast China Clay pit, a strange modern scar on this landscape where humankind has been leaving its mark in more subtle ways for millennia.

Keep to the path, ignoring the first footbridge to your left. After about 1.5km, you'll reach a second footbridge. Cross the ditch here and locate a boundary stone about 50m beyond it. Looking to the northeast you will see the stony head of Shell Top – head directly towards this, across open moor.

After about 400m of steady climbing you will reach another boundary stone,

which sits at the entrance of the rubbly remains of an ancient settlement. Wander through this enigmatic and little-known site, imagining what life might have been like here 3000 years ago, and continue climbing to Shell Top, from where Dartmoor lays bare, in all its wild and wide-open glory.

The Plym and Erme are reborn here every day, as the vast spongy moor absorbs morning moisture and regular rain showers, and releases the water into streams that combine to become mighty rivers, which wend and bend and carve their way to the South Devon Coast.

From the distinctive rocks of Shell Top, an obvious path leads across the high plateau to a trig point at the unnamed high point of Lee Moor. From here, you can clearly see the rocky top of Trowlesworthy Tor below to your west. Descend across open moor ground to this point, and then continue down to pick up your original path which leads back through the warren to your car.

The Dewerstone dare

Distance **7km** Time **2 hours**
Terrain **woodland trails, open moor**
Map **OS Explorer OL20 or 28**
Access **bus (59) from Plymouth to Shaugh
Bridge; parking in Shaugh Bridge
National Trust car park (free)**

**This short loop has it all: delightful
riverside trails, a myth-infused rocky
crag, stone bridges and an evocative
open stretch of moorland, complete with
wild ponies, ancient stone circles and
800-year-old crosses.**

Just northwest of Shaugh Prior towards
Clearbrook lies Shaugh Bridge. Start at the
National Trust car park, which occupies a
site backed by the remains of a historic clay
kiln. Pass through the gate and cross the
footbridge to reach a V-shaped piece of land
created by the confluence of the Meavy
and Plym Rivers.

Follow the well-formed double-track to
the right, which goes against the flow of
the Plym, ascending up and away from the
cascading water, deep into the dark heart
of Dewerstone Wood. At an elbow in the
track you will see a junction leading to the
Dewerstone itself – this is a diversion, but
it's worth a look if you're interested in
climbing and/or spooky myths.

The trail leads to a large granite outcrop,
the Dewerstone, a popular rock-climbing
crag. According to legend, the Dewer, *aka*
the Wisht Huntsman, is an incarnation of
the Devil who, along with a pack of
phantom hunting hounds, is rumoured to
terrorise the moor here after dark, so don't
delay too long.

Return to the main path and continue to
climb the cobbled track, which was once
used as a tramway for transporting granite
from the quarries that pockmark the hill.

Look out for a steep narrow path leading away from the main track, and follow this up through the trees until you emerge at a stony tor top, overlooking Wigford Down.

Standing on the stones, you will see several paths leading northeast. Pick the middle or right-hand path, and try and spot a weather-worn headless cross to your left as you walk across the down. Keep a stone wall on your right as you traverse the moor, and shadow the wall as it begins to descend towards the river.

Near the bottom is another cross – this one fully restored. About 100m further down you'll encounter a track; follow this left until you meet the road and see Cadover Bridge just to your right. Cross the bridge (watching out for cars), then turn immediately right to follow the flow of the River Plym through the car park. This is a

popular picnic and paddling spot, and if you're lucky there'll be an ice-cream van waiting for you.

Locate the gate and pick up the Pipe Track – named after the irrigation pipe that lines its length. From here, a path wends through North Wood and West Down, sometimes dipping tantalisingly close to the chattering river, but eventually climbing away from the water and diving deeper into the forest. Glance right to spot climbers clinging to the Dewerstone on the other side of the valley.

When the path splits at an old concrete structure, take the right fork and follow it almost to the road. Just before you get there, another right turn takes you along a permissive footpath, down some steps and back into the car park.

Gibbet Hill and the Leaning Tower

Distance 9.25km **Time** 3 hours
Terrain open moor **Map** OS Landranger
201 (or OS Explorer 112 and OL28)
Access parking in Lydford Gorge National
Trust car park (free)

Lydford Gorge is one of Dartmoor's
premier natural attractions, and the
3.5km walk around the woodlands and
waterfalls of the National Trust site is
highly recommended. But Lydford is also
a door to the moor, and this free-range
wander on the wild side takes you from
the rim of the gorge, through the haunted
history of Gibbet Hill and over to the
enigmatic Leaning Tower of Dartmoor.

Start at the car park at the Waterfall End
of the gorge – named for the stunning
30m White Lady Waterfall, the biggest
cascade in the South West, which plunges
into the gorge just beyond the National
Trust gate.

Head away from the gorge, turn left and,
ignoring the first path on the right, cross
the bridge over the old railway. Then turn
right to join the West Devon Way, also
signposted as National Route 27 (part of
the Sustrans National Cycle Network).

Pass through a gate, turn right again
and follow the route of the West Devon
Way as it shadows a fenceline along a
bumpy bit of bridleway at the base of the
Black Down hills, once the haunt of
highwaymen who preyed on travellers
riding between Okehampton and
Tavistock. As the path leaves the fence
and starts to ascend the hill, look up to
the iconic church on Brent Tor, which sits
majestically on the mid horizon directly
in front.

Keep walking in the direction of the
distant tor for about 1km, until you reach
a crossroads in the path on the outskirts
of North Brentor village. Swing left and
begin the steep ascent to the top of
Gibbet Hill – if you lose the path, just aim

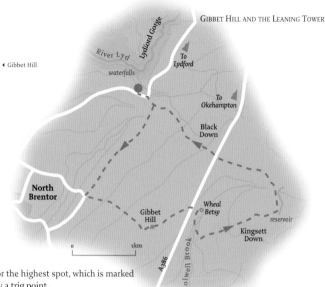

◀ Gibbet Hill

River Lyd

Lydford Gorge

waterfalls

To Lydford

To Okehampton

Black Down

North Brentor

Gibbet Hill

Wheal Betsy

reservoir

Kingsett Down

A386

Cholwell Brook

0   1km

for the highest spot, which is marked by a trig point.

This hill's name betrays its horrible history. Centuries ago, Lydford Castle was an infamous prison and the town had a grim reputation as a place where harsh justice was dealt out. It is said that when highwaymen and other villains were apprehended, they were executed and their bodies left to rot in a gibbet (suspended metal cage) on the top of this hill to deter other potential ne'er-do-wells from joining the dark side. This practice has bequeathed the summit an ominous atmosphere, even on a fine day, but the views are far-reaching, across Brent Tor and the wide wild moor.

Take the long drop off the summit by continuing northeast, aiming for the wonky chimney of Wheal Betsy, a historic lead-silver mine that's better known to

drivers along the A386 as the Leaning Tower of Dartmoor. To reach the National Trust–protected ruin, carefully cross the main road via a couple of opposing gates.

Bidding Betsy goodbye, follow the footpath up over Kingsett Down until you meet a T-junction in the track, close to a reservoir building. Turn left and continue around the contour of the hill to another gate leading back across the A386.

Once across the road, Brent Tor will again be visible away to your left, looking over the stooped shoulder of Gibbet Hill. Aim at the big white house directly in front of you, and follow the path as it descends Black Down back to the gate, which leads to the bridge and the gorge car park.

The Taw by the Tarka Trail

Distance 11.5km **Time** 3 hours 30
Terrain riverside paths, open moor,
country lanes **Map** OS Explorer OL28
Access parking in Finch Foundry National
Trust car park in Sticklepath

**This north Dartmoor walk follows in the
otter prints of the Tarka Trail as it ducks
through verdant woodlands and dives
back and forth across the River Taw,
before boldly heading out onto the
open moor, beneath the brow of Scarey
Tor, crossing Belstone Common and
climbing Cosdon Hill.**

The very top of Dartmoor is visible from
here, with 619m Yes Tor and 621m High
Willhays only a few kilometres away, but
often out of bounds behind the red flags
that warn of army activity. This walk is
safe, but – as always on the periphery of
Dartmoor's Danger Zone – if you see
something unusual, don't pick it up; it
could be unexploded ordnance.

From the south end of the Finch
Foundry car park in the village of
Sticklepath, 6km east of Okehampton,
cross the babbling Taw and turn right to
follow the river that still turns the wheels
of the historic Finch Foundry, the
country's last working water-powered
forge, which was capable of turning out
400 tools a day when it was in full flow.

Stick by the river as you stroll through
leafy Skaigh Wood and Belstone Cleave,
crossing bridges inscribed with wonderful
words from Henry Williamson's famous
novel, *Tarka the Otter*. The full Tarka Trail
is 290km long, but this is one of its
prettiest sections.

After about 2km, you cross the river
and turn right up a little incline into the
village of Belstone. Take a left opposite
the church and climb out of town towards
Watchet Hill. At the end of the sealed
road, you pass through a gate and
enter the moor proper. Pick up a

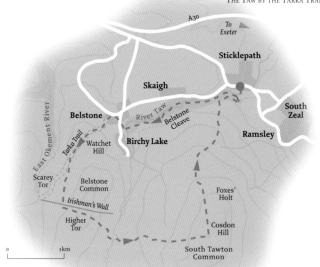

bridleway and keep walking southwest.

The Tarka Trail soon takes a right fork to descend and cross the East Okement River, but ignore that and continue along the contour line until you stumble across the remains of the mysterious Irishman's Wall. The exact history of this wall has become clouded over time – stories suggest it was built by Irish labourers to enclose a part of Dartmoor, but local men pushed it over in defiance.

Like the ruined wall, you need to climb – up onto the summit of Belstone Common, between Belstone and Higher Tors, where a series of impressive boulders provide a vantage point for 360-degree views around the vast moorscape.

Drop off the summit and pick out a track at the bottom of the hill, which leads to a ford just beneath Higher Tor that might allow you to cross the River Taw without getting your boots wet (depending on your balance, and the water level). Once across, ascend due east across open pathless moor, aiming for the high point of Cosdon Hill, where you'll find a beacon and cairn.

A path leads north down off the hill. Avoid the right turn shooting towards South Zeal, and keep heading down until you cross a wall and gate to pick up another path leading to Skaigh Wood, where you turn right and follow a narrow path through the trees to Finch Foundry.

Fingle Bridge from Castle Drogo

Distance **6.5km** Time **2 hours**
Terrain **forest footpaths, riverside trails, short section of quiet country road**
Map **OS Explorer OL28** Access **weekday bus (173) from Exeter Bus/Train Station to the bottom of Castle Drogo's drive, 800m from the start; parking at Castle Drogo National Trust car park (free)**

This River Teign–tracing trek is one of Dartmoor's most popular walks, and for very good reason. From a start point in the grounds of the last castle to be built in Britain, it follows a section of the Two Moors Way over the shoulder of a tor with terrific views before dropping down to the riverbank, straight into the arms of one of the moor's most amazing pubs. If you can tear yourself away from the beer garden, walk waterside almost all the way back.

The easy to follow route starts in the forecourt of Castle Drogo, 2km from Drewsteignton village centre. Despite its marvellously medieval-sounding moniker, this country pile was only completed in 1930. Now a National Trust property, it is well equipped with a café, toilets and a car park – which is where you begin.

Head up the drive, following Hunter's Path signs. Walk down a set of steps and swing left at the bottom, picking up signs for Fingle Bridge and making your way across the excellently named Piddledown Common. Very shortly you will come to Sharp Tor, which delivers an eye-watering valley vista.

Carry on through Hunting Gate to a path that descends across Drewston Common. When the path meets the road, hook a right and wander 100m downhill to Fingle Bridge and the beguiling inn that now bears the same name (having previously been called The Angler's Rest).

Picturesquely positioned on the

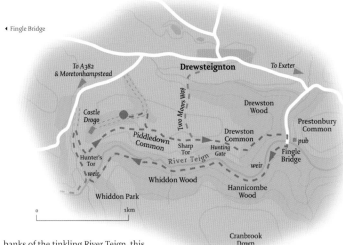

◄ Fingle Bridge

To A382 & Moretonhampstead

Drewsteignton

To Exeter

Castle Drogo

Two Moors Way

Drewston Wood

Prestonbury Common

Piddledown Common

Sharp Tor

Drewston Common

Hunting Gate

pub

Hunter's Tor

River Teign

Fingle Bridge

weir

weir

Whiddon Wood

Hannicombe Wood

Whiddon Park

Cranbrook Down

0   1km

banks of the tinkling River Teign, this country pub's beer garden boasts a lovely perspective of the river and the famous bridge, which dates to the 17th century. The inn began life as a teahouse at the end of the 19th century, but soon moved on to stronger stuff – it's almost impossible not to go in for a quick libation, but don't linger too long because there's plenty more to enjoy on this walk.

While you wet your whistle, make a decision about whether to cross the bridge or not – paths hug the Teign on both banks in the direction you need to go. The described route crosses the river, but if you prefer not to you can simply turn right at the river's edge and follow the Fisherman's Path west.

If, however, you choose to cross the bridge, turn right as soon as you're over, meander through the meadow, cross a

wooden bridge and pick up a path called the Forester's Track. This leads along the riverbank, past a hydroelectric plant and through the Tudor-era Whiddon Deer Park which was created 500 years ago to enclose a herd of fallow deer (creatures you may very well see during your walk).

Shortly after leaving the deer park, you cross a little suspension bridge and the track joins with the Fisherman's Path on the north bank of the river. If the water is high, it's worth checking out the weir, 100m or so downstream. Otherwise, after crossing the bridge, join a section of the Two Moors Way heading north (straight ahead) towards Hunter's Tor and back into the grounds of Castle Drogo – where that café awaits.

Mardon Down and the Teign Valley

Distance 13.5km **Time** 4 hours
Terrain riverside paths, open moor, quiet
country lanes **Map** OS Explorer OL28
Access parking at Bridford Wood National
Trust car park (free)

**From the shelter of the leafy Teign Valley
to the wild windblown top of Mardon
Down, this walk links a series of
wonderful woods with evocative open
moorland via riverside paths, rural
villages, ancient stone circles and the
famous Headless Cross.**

From the car park in Bridford Wood, 2km
southwest of the village of Dunsford, walk
down towards the river – watching out for
cars – and cross the small bridge. Turn left
as soon as you're across the water, and pick
up the path running alongside the
babbling River Teign, which is busy
rushing in the other direction.

Stick to this delightful single-track
path as it tightly hugs the riverbank for
around 2.5km, until you meet the junction
with Boyland Road. Join this quiet road for
around 750m as it climbs to the small
village of Clifford. Turn left at the
crossroads, cross the river at Clifford Bridge
and then, when the road splits, take the
right fork.

After about 100m, a footpath leads left
from the road; follow this as it shadows a
stream up through Halls Cleave. Myriad
trails spider through these woods, but
stick to the main path and keep climbing
as it wends west and then south to bring
you out on Mardon Down.

Cross the road, pick up the path again
and you'll soon spot the unmistakable
form of the Headless Cross. Despite its
name, this feature – also known as the
Maximajor Stone – was never a cross and it

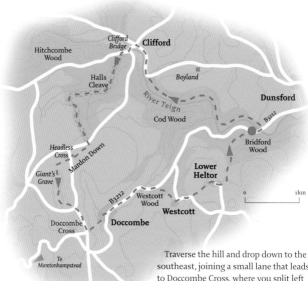

never had a head to lose; it's a megalith (a relatively recent replacement for the original, which had survived from prehistoric times only for someone to drive a car into it).

Continue past this prominent standing stone and cross another road, still heading uphill. Look out for a distinct stone circle on your right as you climb, and soon you will be amid more cairns and boulders on a spot known as the Giant's Grave – the burial place, according to local legend, of a giant named Maximajor, who subsequently rose from the dead.

Traverse the hill and drop down to the southeast, joining a small lane that leads to Doccombe Cross, where you split left and follow a bridleway into Doccombe itself. Walk through the village, pick up the B3212 and walk carefully along the road for almost 1km, until you reach a footpath branching right through Westcott Wood. Follow this path as it climbs to the small hamlet of Westcott.

Take the road travelling uphill from the village and after about 200m pick up the footpath leading to Heltor. Keep following this path as it doglegs through the tiny village, and then leads you all the way back into Bridford Wood. The walk finishes with a steep descent through the trees to take you back to your car.

Bovey Valley

Distance 17.5km **Time** 5 hours
Terrain riverside trails, forest footpaths,
moorland, quiet roads **Map** OS Explorer
OL28 **Access** bus (39) from Exeter and
Newton Abbot to Bovey Tracey, about 1km
from the start; parking at Parke Estate
National Trust car park (parking charge)

This is a day-long Dartmoor adventure,
which rewards with river-hugging and
tree-lined trails, Iron Age remains and
glorious moor and tor vistas. If you're
short of time or energy, there's an obvious
cheat route in Lustleigh Cleave, which
slices a third of the distance off, but also
cuts out the most dramatic views.

From the car park (about 1km west of the
centre of Bovey Tracey), stroll through
Parke Estate past the Home Farm Café.
Cross the River Bovey and turn left (west)
along the bank to enjoy a sublime riverside
path through Parke Wood.

After 1.5km, leave the river and ascend

some stairs to a rail trail. Follow this cycle
path/walkway west until it meets the road.
Walk a short distance on the quiet road,
turn left at Little Knowle, go under the old
railway bridge and take the first right. After
150m, take the footpath on your left.

Cross a meadow and rejoin the river until
you enter Hisley Wood. Climbing steadily
away from the water, follow an undulating
bridleway until you reach the second major
split in the path. (For a shorter route, go
left here, descend to the bridge, and skip
the next four paragraphs.)

To follow the described route, take the
right fork and climb north towards
Hammerslake, looking out for stone circles
on your way. At a junction near the top,
turn left and ascend a little more to
Sharpitor. Continue to Lustleigh Cleave,
walking past the old location of the
Nutcrackers Logan Stone, which was
toppled into the valley in the 1950s. Shortly
you emerge onto a picturesque plateau

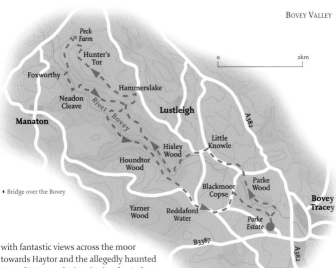

◀ Bridge over the Bovey

with fantastic views across the moor towards Haytor and the allegedly haunted Hound Tor, spooky inspiration for Arthur Conan Doyle's *Hound of the Baskervilles*.

Trace the ridgeline northwest, past Harton Chest and Raven's Tor to dramatic Hunter's Tor, where you'll discover the remains of an Iron Age fort. Cross a stile here and zigzag down the footpath to Peck Farm.

Walk through the farm, following footpath signposts downhill (south) to the pretty little hamlet of Foxworthy, and cross the bridge over the river. Climbing into the woods on the other side, take the first left and walk along a beautiful section of track through Neadon Cleave.

At the next T-junction, turn left and descend to the river. Follow the path and cross the water via the obvious – but nonetheless exciting – giant stepping stones. Once across, turn left briefly, before finding the track leading northeast,

which joins the main bridleway. Turn right and walk east until you meet a junction that you passed earlier. Go right here.

Descend the path to the river and cross the footbridge. Hang a left and walk along the beautiful riverbanks, through the lower reaches of atmospheric Houndtor Wood.

After about 1km, a little switchback merges the footpath with a bridleway, which soon meets a sealed road at Reddaford Water. Follow the road until it splits after about 300m. Take the left fork, turning left again after another 300m. Follow this small road until you see a footpath leading off to the right, into National Trust property at Blackmoor Copse. Follow the trails back to Parke.

Grimspound and Widecombe in the Moor

Distance 12.5km **Time** 3 hours
Terrain open moor, quiet country roads
Map OS Explorer OL28 **Access** Haytor
Hoppa bus (summer Saturdays only)
from Newton Abbot and Bovey Tracey to
Widecombe; parking in Widecombe car
park (parking charge)

**This beguiling circuit takes walkers
deep into prehistoric Dartmoor to the
door of the ancient settlement of
Grimspound and past numerous cairns
and stone circles, which have punctuated
this extraordinary landscape for
millennia. Wild ponies patrol the
route, which traces sections of the
Two Moors Way with views across the
open moor to Hound Tor and Haytor. The
top of Hamel Down is very exposed, so
rug up and prepare to be hit with
anything, from snowstorms to sunburn.**

The walk sets off from Widecombe in
the Moor, where attractions include the

Sexton's Cottage and Church House. From
the car park, follow the road out of the
village towards the hills, travelling
northwest. After about 200m, a footpath
leads away from the road on the left and
quickly ascends the steep flanks of Hamel
Down, via Kingshead.

After snaking around the fields a little,
the trail soon meets the Two Moors Way.
Turn right to join this path as it runs
along the ridgeline of Hamel Down, going
past several cairns, burrows and crosses
which have studded the hill for
thousands of years. If the day is fine, look
to the east for good views of Hound Tor
and Haytor. At the highest point of the
hill, close to the much-weathered remains
of Hamel Down Cross, the path forks; take
the left track, staying on the route of the
Two Moors Way, and head for Hameldown
Tor cairn.

The path descends suddenly from here,
plunging you unexpectedly into an arena

◀ Wild horse on Hamel Down

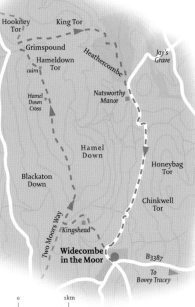

of standing stones and mounds, encircled by a ring of rocks. This is Grimspound – a Bronze Age village, consisting of 24 hut circles, tucked between Hookney and Hameldown Tors. First settled around 1300BC, this site was excavated in the 19th century, but it remains something of an enigma. You can freely explore the site, which is completely open to the public and the elements. Walking into this ancient place in the middle of the moor is quite a surreal experience – compared to the costs and crowds encountered at Stonehenge, the scene is tranquil to the point of loneliness.

Once you've exhausted your inner Indiana Jones, walk east across the downs to King Tor. Stay left when the trail forks, and descend into the valley via a footpath that leads towards a copse of trees, called Heathercombe, which has a small stream running through its midst. Turn right when you meet a junction, and follow the path through the woods towards Natsworthy Manor to meet a road.

An interesting detour here (about 1km each way) takes you to Jay's Grave, the quiet roadside resting place of a young woman who, according to local legend, tragically took her own life in the 18th century. Several myths and ghost stories surround this site, fuelled by the

fact that there are always fresh flowers on the grave and nobody knows who places them there.

Back on the main route, you will see Widecombe in the Moor's iconic Church of Saint Pancras directly in front of you. Also known as the Cathedral of the Moor, this attractive square tower is your target as you stroll the final 3km back into the village, passing Honeybag and Chinkwell Tors on your left. The road is quiet, but exercise caution if you hear cars approaching.

Holne Woods to Sharrah Pool

Distance 7km Time 2 hours
Terrain woodland and riverside trails
Map OS Explorer OL28 Access parking at
New Bridge in the Dartmoor National
Park Authority car park (donations)

An out-and-back path that leads through
wonderful oak woodlands along the
banks of the rampaging River Dart to
a wild-swimming spot at Sharrah Pool –
complete with waterfalls and a little
sandy beach – perfect for a splash around
on a summer's day, or a secluded picnic
at any time.

Start at the car park at New Bridge, just
north of Holne and west of Ashburton,
where you'll find toilets and good
information boards about local flora and
fauna. Carefully cross the river via the
stone bridge. Turn right into the trees and
join the Two Moors Way as it heads
towards Holne through Cleave Wood.

The twists and turns of the Dart
delight to your right, as the river charges
recklessly around rocks and over drops,
including the scenic Horseshoe Falls.
After about 750m, at a Y-junction, bid the
Two Moors Way farewell, take the right
fork and follow the river along a well-
formed track.

Pass through a gate into Holne
Woods, and walk on through a verdant
forestscape along a path lined with
magical moss-covered rocks. The route
takes you beneath a waterfall and across
a small stream via strategically placed
stepping stones.

The path rises over a hill before
dropping back down to water level, and
you have the option of taking a small path
that skirts closer to the river, or following
the main path – the two strands join up
again after about 500m anyway, and both
lead to the same place: Sharrah Pool.

◄ Sharrah Pool

Passing through a gate you descend to an idyllic spot, where a small sandy beach leads out into a calm stretch of water, about 100m long, between two gentle sets of rapids. This is Sharrah Pool – a renowned wild swimming spot which, despite its popularity, still makes you feel as though you've discovered a fantastic secret if you're lucky enough to get it to yourself on a sun-splashed day. The slow-moving water is about chest-deep on an average-sized adult, and the area is dotted with sunbathing rocks, specially arranged for you by serendipity.

Picnic and play here to your heart's content, and then return the way you came (the path peters out 50m beyond the pool – so it's impossible to do a through-route). On the way back, consider branching right at the junction with the Two Moors Way to explore the lovely village of Holne, with its charismatic Church House Inn, parts of which date back to the 14th century.

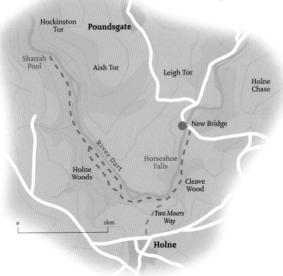

Hockinston Tor

Poundsgate

Sharrah Pool

Aish Tor

Leigh Tor

Holne Chase

New Bridge

River Dart

Horseshoe Falls

Holne Woods

Cleave Wood

Two Moors Way

0   1km

Holne

Hembury Woods

Distance 6.5km (short version 5km)
Time 1 hour 30 Terrain woodland and
riverside trails Map OS Explorer OL28
Access parking in the Hembury Woods
National Trust car park (free)

A lovely looping route along the banks of the River Dart and through an ancient English oak forest to a hilltop where the remains of a medieval castle hide within the embrace of an Iron Age fort. This walk offers plenty of river paddling and waterside picnic opportunities on warm days, fantastic woodland colours in autumn and spring, and seasonal flowers such as bluebells and wild garlic.

Hembury Woods is west of the A38 between Buckfastleigh and Ashburton. From the leafy surrounds of the National Trust car park to the south of the fort,

carefully cross the road and pick up the path leading straight ahead into Hembury Woods. After about 100m you'll reach a crossroads in the track, with a sign pointing left for the fort and straight on for the river. Take the latter.

When you reach the playful river, turn left and hug the bank for the next 1km. If the sun is out, this is an especially magical place, where the light shimmies its way through the trees to dance on the river's ripples, and the boughs extending over the water are alive with the activities of wagtails and nuthatches.

You cross several streams along the way, but once you reach one with no obvious stepping stones or bridge, it's time to turn your back on the water and climb into the heart of the oak forest to explore.

At a Y-junction, stick to the main path

◀ River Dart

(left), take a deep breath and start climbing. This is the steepest section of the walk, but thankfully it's quite short. At the next T-junction, turn right and stay right when the trail splits again, ascending until you reach a stile at the edge of the woods. Climb this and go through a gate a few yards further on.

Walking south now, cross another gate/stile and pass a ruined barn on your right. Keep going, through another gate, until you reach the entrance to Hembury Castle, the remains of a prehistoric hillfort that dates back at least 2000 years, cleverly built on a spot that commands incredible views across the Dart Valley and east Dartmoor.

You can do a 1km circuit of the outer defensive ring that surrounds the fort, or stroll right through the middle of the site, passing over the central mound which is actually the remains of a medieval castle built within the bigger, older prehistoric fort.

Leave the site via the southeastern gate and rejoin the path heading south. At the next T-junction, turn left and follow signposts pointing to the car park, threading through oak, silver birch, holly and hazel trees via a series of switchbacks.

Map labels: Staddicombe, Southpark Wood, ruin, Hembury Woods, Hembury Castle, Shere Wood, Blackmoor Wood, Holy Brook, River Dart, North Wood, To Buckfastleigh, To Buckfast, 0 500m

At the next T-junction, either turn left and take the quick route back to the car park, or go straight on until you reach the road. Carefully cross, pick up the path again and follow it right, through more mixed woodland. After about 750m, take a sharp left and descend along a distinct path to the banks of Holy Brook. The path remains flat from here, tracing the stream, until you turn left just before the road and climb a distance of 100m or so back to the car park.

Despite the protective influence of Ireland and the Bristol Channel, Devon's north shore still feels the fury of the tempestuous Atlantic when the weather gets wild and, as a result, there's a marked contrast between the county's coastlines.

The combes and coves on the north coast have a serrated edge to them, with a sensational savagery to the shorefront during storms when snarling waves reveal ship-snaring rocky teeth below cliffs that erupt out of the sea. Even the folklore and fiction of the region has dark undertones, with stories of wreckers around Mortehoe and cave-dwelling cannibals at Clovelly.

But you'll also find soft sand and superb surf here, most notably on the dune-backed beaches of Woolacombe and Putsborough, where kids and dogs can safely run wild as you stroll the coastal path. On the walks that explore Heddon Mouth, the Hartland Peninsula and Peppercombe, trails thread through verdant valleys and clifftop copses. Seals can often be seen in the bays below and you might spot playful harbour porpoises or even a strange sunfish.

The coastal settlements here are as charismatic as they are postcard cute. Historic harbour towns such as Ilfracombe and fishing villages with cobbled streets and antiquated alehouses, like Clovelly, quietly went about their business for centuries, blissfully unaware of how special they were, until the visitors arrived.

By the time local authors such as Charles Kingsley (*Westward Ho!*, *The Water-Babies*) and Henry Williamson (*Tarka the Otter*) started evocatively describing their surrounds, word was well and truly out, and once awakened the tourism industry went into overdrive. Now, North Devon sees an annual influx of millions of visitors each summer, and celebrities such as Damien Hirst have set up residence and left their mark – Hirst's 20m *Verity* overlooks Ilfracombe Harbour, giving the old town a very contemporary edge.

Out of holiday season, you'll often find beaches and headlands deserted, however, but even at the height of summer, the one way to experience the best bits of this coast without the crowds is to walk.

The Hartland Peninsula ▶

North Devon

Hartland Peninsula

Distance 13.5km **Time** 4 hours
Terrain woodland paths, quiet country
lanes, exposed coastal and clifftop trails
Map OS Explorer OL126 **Access** parking in
Hartland car park (parking charge)

The Hartland Peninsula is North Devon at
its brutally beautiful best. During this
walk, the coast-hugging footpath tiptoes
almost alarmingly close to incredible
cliffs that fall away to reveal fang-like
rocks, snarling and gnashing away at the
relentless Atlantic rollers in an explosive
frenzy of foam. Countless ships have
come to grief on this jagged shoreline
over the centuries, and a lighthouse has
stood sentinel at Hartland since 1874.
Below, in the nape of Barley Bay, it's
common to see seals playing and fishing
between the rocks, masters of their
dramatic domain.

This path goes very close to some
precipitous plunges, with no view-
spoiling barriers in place – be very aware

of this if walking with young children or
dogs (both best kept on leads during the
first section between Hartland Quay and
the lighthouse) or if you're walking in
poor visibility (not advised).

From the car park in Hartland village,
walk past the Hart Inn, cross North Street
and follow West Street as it bends right
towards the tennis courts and playing
fields. As the road forks, keep right and, at
the end of the street, take the footpath
leading left.

Follow this path as it cavorts through
lovely leafy woodlands to Abbey River.
Cross via a footbridge and turn left to
trace the waterway as it flows through
Pattard Wood towards the grounds of
Hartland Abbey. When you hit a lane,
turn left. Cross back over the river and
then turn right to take the road into the
village of Stoke, walking past the site of a
holy well, where the Welsh hermit,

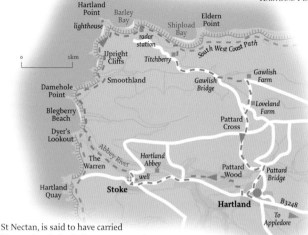

St Nectan, is said to have carried his own head after being set upon and decapitated by a gang of robbers.

Turn right just after the well and skirt around the church, picking up a footpath that leads back to the riverbank and then follows it all the way down to a footbridge at Dyer's Lookout. Historic Hartland Quay is worth a diversion, but this walk crosses the footbridge to begin tracing the coast around Warren and Blegberry Cliffs.

Some stern climbs await as you follow the path on a rollercoaster ride around the headland, through Smoothlands Valley and over the aptly named Upright Cliffs – each ascent richly rewarded with breathtaking vistas. Look out for waterfalls, which lurch in and out of view as you round the cove tops towards Hartland Point Lighthouse.

The lighthouse is closed to the public, but you can explore the headland it occupies. Be sure to scan the waters of Barley Bay below, looking for the bobbing heads of grey seals.

Pass the modern radar station and, when you get to a major junction in the path at Titchberry, about halfway around Shipload Bay, take the bridleway leading away from the coast to your right. At the road, turn left and walk east (ignoring the turning to your right) until you reach Gawlish Bridge.

A footpath here leads across fields to Gawlish Farm, where you turn right and follow a lane through another farm, straight over a crossroads and onwards until you meet a T-junction.

Turn left here and walk to Pattard Cross, where you take a right and then an immediate left to stroll the quiet country lane to Pattard Bridge. Cross Abbey River one last time and walk back into Hartland along West Ball Hill.

◀ Hartland Point Lighthouse

Clovelly

Distance 9.5km **Time** 3 hours
Terrain woodland trails, exposed clifftop
paths, cobbled lanes **Map** OS Explorer
OL126 **Access** bus (319) from Barnstaple
and Bideford to Clovelly; parking in the
Brownsham National Trust car park
(donation welcome)

Lovely Clovelly is a dollop of Devon
heaven. This is the county as it's seen on
a million fridge magnets, but postcard
prettiness comes at a price – one that's
measured in crowds and entry fees. To
visit the famous car-free village, most
people drive or catch a coach/bus to the
visitor centre and pay an entry fee, but
there is another way – you can walk.

This picturesque seaside stroll begins at
a National Trust car park, takes in a
fabulous stretch of the South West Coast
Path and returns through a wonderful
wood, and it doesn't cost a penny.

Leave the little car park in remote
Brownsham via a stile opposite the
entrance, and follow signs indicating the
coast path. Descend through trees to a
T-junction. Left leads down to Windbury
Head, but keep right and walk to
Brownsham Cliff, following signs to
Mouth Mill. These cruel cliffs tease with
occasional sea glimpses, but much of the
early part of this section is through tree-
fringed fields, and you'll have to be
content with hearing the waves. Look out
for raptors such as buzzards here.

At Mouth Mill, the path drops steeply
down to sea level, where you can explore
old limekilns and have a play on pebbly
Mouthmill Beach, with its iconic
Blackchurch Rock backdrop.

Cross the stream, ascend some wooden
steps and follow the trail as it climbs the
steep hill opposite, towards Gallantry
Bower. There are several excellent
viewpoints on this path, but mind your
footing when taking photos – it's a long

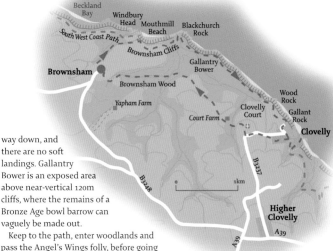

way down, and there are no soft landings. Gallantry Bower is an exposed area above near-vertical 120m cliffs, where the remains of a Bronze Age bowl barrow can vaguely be made out.

Keep to the path, enter woodlands and pass the Angel's Wings folly, before going through a gate and skirting the grounds of Clovelly Court. Stay left and you eventually meet the sealed road, just below the main entrance to Clovelly.

Descend the steep cobbled street into the historic fishing village, made famous (and ultimately super touristy) by local writer Charles Kingsley, author of *Westward Ho!* and *The Water Babies*.

Myriad other yarns surround this ridiculously picturesque village, including one that has King Arthur's magician, Merlin, being born in a cave behind a waterfall just beyond the lifeboat station. Dramatic coastal waterfalls do extend around Clovelly Bay in the area known as the Devil's Kitchen, and another more gory story depicts the caves behind them being populated by cannibals.

Once you've explored the village,

clamber back up the cobbles – sparing a thought for the donkeys that traditionally transported fish and tourists up this hill – and exit through the visitor centre area and main car park. Walk up the road for a few hundred metres, before turning right towards the church, which you pass on your right.

A bridleway branches left, crossing a field and going through the middle of Court Farm. Stick to this track as it traverses another field and then enters beautiful Brownsham Wood, where you thread through birch, oak, willow, ash, holly and hazel trees. Keep an eye out for horseshoe bats and deer here, and listen for barn owls if walking late in the day. The path doglegs across a creek and leads all the way back to Brownsham car park.

◀ Clifftop view looking back over Mouthmill Beach

Peppercombe

Distance 9km **Time** 3 hours
Terrain woodland trails, coastal path,
wild open beach, quiet country lanes
Map OS Explorer OL126 **Access** bus (319)
from Barnstaple to Buck's Cross, 1km
from the start; parking in Buck's Mills
visitor car park (free)

This walk rambles along the rustic
lanes of rural North Devon before
plunging through a beautiful valley to
a wild, windswept and lonely beach
where cars can't go. The trails, when you
reach them, wend through ancient
forests and beneath arches of orchids,
where you'll be captivated by the
butterflies, and the views across to
Lundy Island are breathtaking.

From the car park in Buck's Mills, head
east, picking up a footpath that meanders
through a woodland, shadowing a stream,
before crossing a field leading to a farm at
Lower Worthygate. Walk through the
farm, turning left after the barn to
descend a ramp, and then going left on
the road, before following it around
to the right.

Passing a couple more buildings, follow
the road to a minor crossroads. Ignore the
left turn and instead follow the road as it
hooks right and travels west towards Sloo
Farm. En route you will pass a footpath
leading off to the right – if your inner beer
diviner is twitching, that's because this
trail leads to the Hoops Inn, a famous
thatched pub, full of character.

Assuming you can resist the pull of a
pint, carry on until you reach Northway.
Do a dogleg through the village, turning
left along the road and then right along a
path to enter Peppercombe Woods. (That
diviner will be fidgeting again, because
yet another great pub lies just up at the
top of the valley, the Coach & Horses at

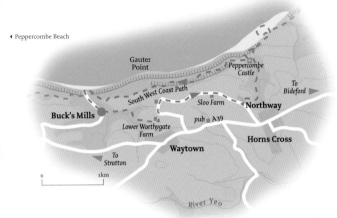

◀ Peppercombe Beach

Horns Cross.) Turn left and descend the steep hill towards the beach.

Although you're ultimately going to be returning along the South West Coast Path in the other direction, it's worth continuing on a little way east to access Peppercombe Beach here.

Reaching the sand can be easier said than done, but follow the orchid-lined path for a few hundred metres and you'll find a way down the sandy cliff to explore a wild open expanse of deserted sand, evocative in its isolation, punctuated by rock pools and strewn with driftwood blown in from the Atlantic.

This is a great spot to gaze across Bideford Bay towards Lundy Island, which lies on the horizon 19km distant across the Bristol Channel. If you find it hard to tear yourself away, it's worth knowing that the National Trust operate a cheap and cheerful basic bothy here at Peppercombe, specifically designed for walkers, where you can literally look at this view from the loo.

Assuming you need to get back to your car, retrace your steps to the South West Coast Path and follow it west, going past what remains of Peppercombe Castle, a 19th-century castellated bolthole built on a site where an Iron Age promontory fort once stood.

Walk on through an ancient oak woodland, which has survived the fellers' axes and saws over the centuries thanks to its remote location. This is a wonderful spot for wildflowers and butterflies.

The sea occasionally teases through the trees and, when you get back to Buck's Mills, you can turn right at the Old Coastguard Cottage to go and explore the historic village's old quay and beach before heading up the footpath and finding your car.

Baggy Point and Putsborough Sands

Distance 11km **Time** 4 hours
Terrain coastal path, exposed in places,
dunes, open beach **Map** OS Explorer OL139
Access bus (21) from Westward Ho!
and Barnstaple to Croyde; parking in
Croyde Bay National Trust car park
(parking charge)

This route sets off from the surfing
mecca of Croyde and takes walkers
around historic Baggy Point to the
dunescape of Putsborough Beach at the
wilder, southern extremity of the 5km-
long golden arc of Woolacombe Sands,
before heading back across the beach and
over the neck of the peninsula. It's a
coastal classic, with great views, picnic
spots and whalebones.

Exit the Croyde Bay National Trust car
park and turn right along the lane,
following a sign indicating Baggy Point.
Pick up the South West Coast Path at the
fork, and keep left at every junction in the
path thereafter. Not long after a private

driveway branches right, you'll pass some
titanic vertebrae – the skeletal remains of
a dead whale, which washed up on Croyde
Beach in 1915.

A little further along, close to a gate,
find a memorial stone dedicated to author
Henry Williamson, who lived most of his
life in nearby Georgeham, where he wrote
the best-known of his many books: *Tarka
the Otter*. Williamson regularly wandered
around this headland and it forms part of
the 209km Tarka Trail.

Keep following the path as it hugs the
peninsula's rocky edge. This wildflower-
fringed section changes complexion
throughout the year – it's cacophonously
chaotic with nesting seabirds in spring,
when the hills blush with flowering
gorse, idyllic throughout the summer
months, busy with birds again during
autumn, as migratory species prepare to
fly south, and wonderfully wild in winter,
with waves and wind gusts roaring in
from across the Atlantic.

used when conditions were too rough to launch lifeboats.

Follow the path over the high point of the peninsula – with great views along Woolacombe Sands – and past the remains of old Second World War pillboxes, built to train troops ahead of Operation Overlord and the D-Day landings. The gorse grows high here as you follow signs for Woolacombe and the South West Coast Path to a gate opening onto the road. Go through and turn left. Ignore the sign for Putsborough and continue straight ahead as the road narrows and segues into a bridleway.

At a three-way junction, where a signpost indicates Woolacombe (straight ahead) and Putsborough (back the way you've come), take the third option for the Coast Path, turning left through the dunes. Descend to the beach and walk back across the sand towards Baggy Point.

At Putsborough you'll see steps leading to the car park, next to a shop and café. Climb these, turn right on the road and retrace your footsteps. Pass back through the gate you came through earlier, and take the left fork to follow a public footpath – past a prehistoric standing stone – across the bottom of the peninsula and back towards Croyde Beach and the car park.

Look out for birds of prey, such as merlin and peregrine, and glance down to search for seals frolicking and fishing around the rocks. At one point you can descend to the shoreline to explore the rockpools.

When you reach Baggy Point, inhale the fantastic view – Hartland Peninsula is to your left, Morte Point to your right and straight ahead across the Bristol Channel lies lovely Lundy Island.

Turn right, pass through a gate and stick tight to the grassy path that leads left along the edge of the cliff (take care here, especially with children). There's an old wreck post here, once employed by coastguards to practise a rescue technique

Morte Point

Distance **11.2km** Time **3 hours**
Terrain **coastal paths, country lanes and woodland trails; some steps**
Map **OS Explorer 139 (or Explorer OL9)**
Access **bus (303) from Barnstaple to Mortehoe; parking in Mortehoe (parking charge)**

Scenically situated between the seaside resorts of Woolacombe and Ilfracombe, and punctuated by several secret coves and hidden beaches once used by smugglers, Morte Point is a dramatic North Devon peninsula that teases and pleases many walkers and wilderness lovers. But for all its sublime beauty, the area has a dark past.

'Morte' is Latin for death, and this serrated dagger of land earned its macabre moniker during the age of sail, when countless ships came to grief on the rocks just offshore. Five went down here in the winter of 1852 alone and bands of wreckers, including an infamous local character called Elizabeth Berry, would lie in wait for any bounty washed ashore.

Thankfully, it's much safer now – thanks to a lighthouse – but clues to the region's history remain, not least in the name of Mortehoe's excellent local pub, The Ship Aground, where this route starts and finishes. During this walk you will experience some of Devon's most stunning coastline and stroll along one of the best sections of the South West Coast Path (also part of the long-distance Tarka Trail).

About 100m down the road from the pub (in the direction of Woolacombe), take the gate on your right onto a National Trust footpath and continue descending towards Grunta Beach – the northern end of Woolacombe Sands. Before the beach, bear right and trace the water's edge out along the peninsula to Morte Point.

Pensport Rock · Sandy Cove · Lee Bay · **Lee**
Bull Point · lighthouse
Wrinkle Wood · To Ilfracombe
Rockham Bay
Whiting Cove
South West Coast Path
Damage Barton
Rashley's Cleave
Morte Point
Mortehoe
Yarde Farm
Warcombe Lane
Grunta Beach
Burricane Beach
Woolacombe
0 · 1km
Woolacombe Sands
B3343

As you round the point and begin heading east towards Whiting Cove, watch out for seals, which can often be seen cavorting in the water and sunning themselves on rocks around this sheltered shoulder of Rockham Bay. Walk on, around a collection of coves, until you reach a set of steps.

An undulating section of the route begins here, rising up over several hills and dropping down again to cross streams in between them. The views are worth every bit of effort, however. At Bull Point the lighthouse (relocated here in the 1970s from its previous perch near Mortehoe) winks at Wales across the Bristol Channel.

A treat awaits at Sandy Cove; steps lead down to a sheltered beach, where the water is often gin clear and mirror calm – perfect for a dip on sunny summer days. One more short climb sees you join the road. Turn left and take the first right just before reaching the village of Lee.

After 300m, take the footpath to the right, cross a stream and enter a verdant forest full of birdsong. Keeping the stream on your left, wander through Wrinkle Wood, Doctor's Cleave and Rashley's Cleave to Six Acre Wood.

At a T-junction, take the right fork and climb steeply through the ancient woodland. Cross Warcombe Lane and follow the footpath through fields to Damage Barton, turning left at a T-junction in the path and left again onto a lane. Follow this lane for 50m or so before turning right onto another path, which passes through Yarde and leads back into Mortehoe, where The Ship Aground waits to welcome thirsty walkers.

◀ Grunta Beach from Mortehoe

The Ilfracombe Elephant

Distance 4.5km **Time** 1 hour 30
Terrain coastal path, beach, harbourside
streets **Map** OS Explorer OL9
Access bus (301) from Barnstaple and
Combe Martin to Hele Bay; parking at
Hele Bay car park (parking charge)

**Antiquity and modern art collide on
Ilfracombe Harbour in spectacular
fashion, with Damien Hirst's 20m-high
sword-wielding statue of a very pregnant
Verity dominating the skyline of an old
fishing village that features in the 1086
Domesday Book as *Alfriencoma* (Alfred's
Combe). But the area's history stretches
back much further than the Normans,
as this walk, which begins with
a semi-circuit of a hill named after a
4000-year-old burial chamber, reveals.**

From Hele Bay car park, head towards
the beach and pick up the acorn icon that
denotes you're on the route of the South
West Coast Path. Climb the steps to begin
your exploration of the woody green
dome that is Hillsborough – originally
called Hele's Barrow, a reference to a
Bronze Age tomb discovered here in the
1930s, but more popularly known in these
parts as the Sleeping Elephant.

Myriad tracks and trails spider off in all
directions, but keep following the coast
path as it leads around a series of uphill
switchbacks to a lookout point above
Beacon Point. As the name indicates, a
beacon or lighthouse is thought to have
once stood here, but if it existed in the
18th century it didn't help *The London*,
a transport ship that was wrecked in
Rapparee Cove (below on your right as
you continue the walk) whilst trying to
reach Ilfracombe Harbour in 1796. Interest
in this story was reignited in the 1990s,
two centuries after the tragedy, when
bones were disturbed by the sea.

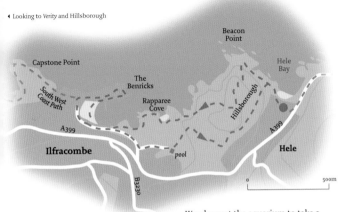

◀ Looking to *Verity* and Hillsborough

Beacon
Point

Hele
Bay

Capstone Point

The
Benricks

South West
Coast Path

Rapparee
Cove

Hillsborough

A399

A399

Ilfracombe

pool

Hele

B3230

0   500m

The path undulates as it approaches the top of the hill, rolling over ridges and ripples in the earth that date to an Iron Age fort that once perched on the peak of this promontory, with a commanding view across the Bristol Channel. Modern visitors can enjoy a very different vista, as they gaze west and take in Hirst's *Verity*, who looks particularly impressive from up here, with a 14th-century chapel right behind her.

At a junction by a hedge, turn right and keep following the South West Coast Path as it drops towards Ilfracombe Harbour. (You can go via the small sandy cove, or stay on the main track.) If the tide is out, cut straight across the harbour, wending between beached boats to reach steps that clamber up the pier. Otherwise, walk around the waterfront.

Wander past the aquarium to take a closer look at *Verity*, a big bronze beauty that becomes all the more extraordinary as you get near enough to make out her finer details, which include, on one side, a depiction of inner organs and an in-utero embryo. Hirst describes his creation – which stands upon several giant law books, carrying a set of scales in her right hand – as a 'modern allegory of truth and justice'.

Round the harbour and continue along the road, taking the third turning on the left (Larkstone Gardens) towards the swimming pool, and then following the footpath to the left of the pool building. Cross the recreation grounds and then turn right when you hit a T-junction in the path. Trace this track back around the hill to the car park, taking the right option each time the path forks.

Heddon Valley to Woody Bay

Distance 8.5km Time **3 hours**
Terrain **woodland trails, coastal paths**
Map **OS Explorer OL9** Access **parking in
the Heddon Valley National Trust car park
(donation welcome)**

**Showing off the gnarly North Devon
shoreline in all its glory, this circular,
cove-caressing route exits Heddon Valley
via a gloriously elevated bridleway –
offering views, bird sightings and a
Roman fort – and returns along a coastal
trail, skimming the dramatic cliffline all
the way back to Heddon's Mouth.**

From the riverside car park at Heddon
Valley, cross the road and go past the
National Trust shop and toilets towards
the unmissable Hunter's Inn. Veer to the
right of the pub, turning immediately off

the road and taking the permissive
bridleway. When this path forks, keep to
the right, staying on the bridleway.

Wander through Road Wood on this
broad trail – a well-made double-track,
optimistically designed as a carriageway
to transport people from steamboats
docking at Woody Bay to the Hunter's Inn.
The track quickly rises out of the treeline
and coils around the curves of the valley.
After crossing Hill Brook the path
presents several stunning viewpoints
where you can gaze over Heddon's Mouth
Beach and out across the Bristol Channel
to Lundy Island.

The vistas continue as you turn the
corner and begin heading east along
the coast, with the Cow and
Calf and Wringapeak

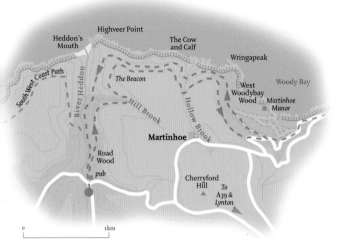

Map with labels: Heddon's Mouth, Highveer Point, The Cow and Calf, Wringapeak, Woody Bay, South West Coast Path, River Heddon, The Beacon, Hill Brook, West Woodybay Wood, Martinhoe Manor, Hollow Brook, Martinhoe, Road Wood, pub, Cherryford Hill, To A39 & Lynton

0 — 1km

before and below you. A small path branches right, leading uphill to the remains of an old Roman fortlet known as The Beacon, which dates to 75AD. All that remains are mounds in the ground, but you can see why the imperialist Italians chose the spot as a lookout and signal station. There's no through route, so you need to return to the main track the way you came.

The trail wends slightly inland and passes through some tree cover as it follows the contours around the combe created by Hollow Brook, before emerging to serve up wonderful views across Woody Bay. (Keep one eye skyward and you may glimpse peregrine falcons and buzzards here.)

When you hit the road, turn left (virtually straight on) and drop down the hill. Take the next left, leaving the road and descending through trees (oak, ash, larch and birch) along a mixed-use track. At a sharp elbow in the track, pick up the footpath (which goes straight ahead) and enter West Woodybay Wood. (Alternatively stick to the road to explore Woody Bay itself.)

This single-track path creeps along the curves of the gorse-, heather- and bracken-covered cliffs, all the way back to Heddon's Mouth, offering spectacular views throughout the journey. You need to concentrate on your footing at times, but don't forget to stop regularly and take in your surrounds – this is one of the finest stretches of the South West Coast Path.

Looking back along the trail to Wringapeak arch

Index